THE ORIGIN OF MISS VICTORY

Evil Bore Not!

Stephen J. Cassinelli

Copyright © 2024 Stephen J. Cassinelli

eBook ISBN: 979-8-8692-6767-2
Paperback ISBN: 979-8-86926768-9
Hardcover ISBN: 979-8-8692-6778-8

All Rights Reserved. Any unauthorized reprint or use of this material is strictly prohibited. No part of this book may be reproduced or transmitted in any form or by any means, electronic or mechanical, including photocopying, recording, or by any information storage and retrieval system without express written permission from the author.

All reasonable attempts have been made to verify the accuracy of the information provided in this publication. Nevertheless, the author assumes no responsibility for any errors and/or omissions.

Table of Contents

DEDICATION — 1
Prologue — 3

Part 1

Chapter 1: Uncovering the Mysteries..6
Chapter 2: A Gift from the Past.. 13

Part 2

Chapter 3: The Hidden Castle's Secrets..22
Chapter 4: The Perfect Specimen...29
Chapter 5: Unveiling Shadows...36

Part 3

Chapter 6: Vanishing Currents...43
Chapter 7: The Birth of Miss Victory.. 49
Chapter 8: Reflections and Reunion...56

Acknowledgments: — 60
Coming Soon: — 61

DEDICATION

For those who have risked and given their lives, past, present, & future, so that others may live free.

Prologue

The Importance of Comic Books and Superheroes during World War II

Thank goodness for the patriotic-minded creators of comic book superheroes who remained keenly aware of global current affairs. They were the visionaries who foresaw the inevitable and responded by weaving tales within their publications—stories that served as warnings to readers, particularly children, long before America entered the impending war. The superheroes, who had recently burst onto the scene amidst the rise of Nazi Germany, unexpectedly found themselves assuming a new role far beyond mere entertainment. In fact, they became staunchly patriotic, embodying strong American values.

Comic books that battled the axis powers instilled in young readers a sense of the enemy long before they faced them on the battlefield. These stories, even within publications intended for a young audience, dared to expose the potential for evil. While much of it may have seemed fantastic, children are fortunately more receptive and adaptive to new concepts and ideas than adults. History has proven that these young adults, who later became soldiers, would rather die than be victims—enslaved and subjected to experiments like lab rats. These imaginative stories vividly depicted the horrors mankind is capable of, presenting astonishing ideas through colorful illustrations, showcasing the true nature of evil and what it takes to eradicate it.

By exposing the extraordinary and malevolent tactics employed by the forces of evil, these creations became an effective weapon against oppression, tyranny, and other forms of inhumane treatment towards fellow human beings. Superheroes and comic books seemingly emerged at the perfect time, as they warned against and combated malevolence, while also espousing patriotism and a love for country to their countless young readers. These very readers would later rise to the occasion, successfully defending the American way of life—cherishing freedom at all costs.

It is this author's opinion that comic books were one of the United States most powerful weapons against tyranny, why else would the government allow and actually encourage their production during a time when resources were scarce and the world was at war?

Part II

Chapter 1: Uncovering the Mysteries

EXTRA!!!! NEWS-FLASH!!!!!!! EXTRA!!!!

Read all about it! -

AMERICA'S FIRST PATRIOTIC SUPERHEROINE

At long last!

Origin discovered!

Who is she? Where did she come from?

As discovered and reported By Stephen Cascianelli, May 1, 2019

Fellow treasure hunters and friends of the superheroes, I have experienced the most amazing find of my life this past winter while searching for antiques and other treasures at a thrift store in Woonsocket, Rhode Island. Yes, I stumbled upon and purchased an early to mid-20th-century travel trunk, still in very good condition but stuck shut thanks to a rusted lock. The reason I purchased the trunk was that there appeared to be something inside. Using my father's famously fast-acting petroleum solvent lubricating oil, I soaked a rag and drenched the lock. After some wiggling and jiggling, and a few whacks with a hammer, I am happy to report that I managed to click the mechanism open without destroying the lock.

As soon as the trunk was opened, a musty odor spewed out—the smell of considerable age, mildew, and mothballs. Wrapped up in a white cotton blanket was what appeared to be an old piece of clothing.

Upon removal, I could see it was in a more old-school style, obviously hand-made, heavily worn women's red, white, and blue outfit—oddly modern, very high quality, and attractively designed. Whomever made it did a great job.

Upon closer examination, the outfit consisted of a long-sleeved flannel top that I first thought to be an old-time sports jersey. However, there were no buttons, numbers, or names stitched on it. Instead, a single white silk star was sewn on the front, dead center. When I lifted the top of the costume out of the trunk and shook the mothballs off, a heavy-duty blue and red cape attached to the back collar dropped down to just below the waist. This is when I assumed that what I found must be a costume of sorts. I was kinda bummed out, thinking this wasn't that great of a find. Obviously, it did get better from there.

Next to emerge was a pair of red leather or possibly vinyl shorts that felt much like an old Heart of the Hide leather baseball glove I used to play ball with. The leather was still quite soft, not dried up or brittle in the least. Attached to the shorts was a thick, heavy-duty, stainless steel-reinforced white leather belt with a large brass buckle. The front of the buckle was covered with shiny red plastic, possibly a Bakelite- type material.

There was also a pair of shiny red leather shoes—very streamlined, sleek, in the art deco style. They looked very futuristic, like something you would see in a sci-fi movie. Really cool-looking.

At the very bottom of the trunk, scattered about, there was a pair of thin red leather gloves tied to, I guess what you would call, a very low-profile double-sided black and white, super-minimalistic masquerade-type mask. Yes, at this time, I was convinced that what I found must have had something to do with a theatrical production or, hopefully, something used in a TV show or better yet, a movie.

As I started to put everything back, a group of folded papers fell out of an inside pocket. Printed in pen across the top middle fold in English, "This is my origin, Miss Victory." I unfolded the papers, and it was a handsomely handwritten letter, quite legible but in a language I couldn't understand, nor positively identify. It was signed on the last page. I set them aside.

My first instinct at this point was to Google Miss Victory, and I was quite surprised to see Miss Victory show up at the top of the first page because I never heard of her. I soon found out that Miss Victory was in fact a patriotic superheroine who appeared during the golden age of comic books, which I am aware began in the late 1930s prior to World War 2. Miss Vic's first exploit was published in the comic book Captain Fearless #1, published by Helnit Publications in August 1941.

When I scrolled down, there appeared a site known as Comic Book Plus that actually shows Miss Victory's very first episode in its entirety from Captain Fearless #1! I couldn't believe what I was looking at on the very first panel of the very first Miss Victory episode. The outfit Miss Victory was wearing and the outfit I had sitting before me appeared to be exactly the same. I assumed that what I found must be a replica, or perhaps a Halloween costume made by a fan of this long-forgotten woman superhero. I was a bit stumped and curious to learn more because I thought I knew or heard of all of the patriotic superheroes, especially females during that time, they were very limited. There was Wonder Woman and Lady Liberty and Miss America and I think there was also a Miss Patriot, but I had never heard of Miss Victory. What I realized at that moment was, I didn't know as much as I thought I did.

I had pretty much forgotten about the suit and was more interested in learning more about Miss Victory. Who was she? Where did she go? Who was she affiliated with? What team was she a part of?

I stayed up, skimming through the exploits that have been documented throughout the 2nd World War. Apparently, when the war came to an end, Miss Victory seemed to have fallen off the map, suddenly disappearing from the front lines of the patriotic superhero movement. Still, I could not find any information as to who Miss Victory was or where she came from. I had come to a dead end, and it was getting late, so I laid down, closed my eyes, and thought I might as well get some sleep. After about two or three minutes, my eyes opened up. The letter! It was already 3 a.m., and I was wired, there was no way I could sleep anyway. My second wind was kicking in and maybe a bit of adrenaline too.

While I was looking at the letter, I jumped on Google and started doing some comparative analysis, researching various languages. I found some similarities, but nothing that would be enough to establish any origin. So, I just started typing the letter as it is into my older computer's translation software, from unknown to English, and there it was! Bavarian. Without further ado, I proceeded to enter the entire letter into the translation app, then forwarded the English version to my email and printed it out.

Everything went as planned. Though a bit discombobulated, the translation was full of what appeared to be typographical errors. I have to admit, I was a bit dumbfounded. Was this fact or fiction? I was about to call it a night when I saw the sun was rising so I put on a fresh pot of coffee. I was on a mission.

As I was reading through the document, I came to realize, this wasn't something written for a production or a comic book, it was something else, much more personal, far more dramatic and a bit sad, almost like an entry into a diary, but too long to be that and it wasn't written in a book, just loose papers, as if the person who wrote it didn't stop until they were finished. I felt I was forcing myself to read it just as much as the author forced themselves to finish what they wanted to say. I had the sense that it was more of a statement, or possibly a testimonial or some sort of an affidavit but it wasn't notarized, though it was handwritten. My spidey senses were tingling fearing the worst until I got through it enough to realize that it wasn't a suicide letter, there's a happy ending. I think this is what they call a holographic type will?

I didn't find any of this information when I was researching earlier. I happened to glance up at the clock and to no surprise, it was already past nine, and my eyelids had been shutting down for the past half hour. The java buzz was gone and I needed to sleep so I put the transcript down and laid down on the couch. I didn't want to undress and get into bed, the mail-man would be around soon and if he had to knock on the door for a signature or had a package, I didn't want him to think I was still in bed past noon.

Without interruption I woke up abruptly, and felt as if I didn't sleep a wink but the clock said 4 o'clock so I must have really needed a rest. I had my clothes on so I checked the mailbox and the mailman certainly came by, there was a town paper and some other insignificant junk mail. I mixed up a glass of cold chocolate milk and made myself a tomato and cheese sandwich. About to lollygag about, I realized while there was still time, I better get on the phone and make a few calls.

Without further ado, I gave the Library of Congress a buzz, and after a solid 20-minute wait, plenty of time to eat my sandwich and check my email, a gentleman answered who identified himself as Martin Baker asking how he could help. Not quite sure where to begin, I started reading aloud from the notes I took earlier that morning. He listened patiently then stopped me when I got to the part about migrating to the United States in 1941 and suggested that I should get off the phone while there's still time and give the United States Immigration Bureau a call, extension 1941 and tell them exactly what I told him.

I went ahead and made the call and wouldn't you know it, the phone was answered before I heard it ring once! A young man, who was eating something, mumbled, "Records, can I help you". With little time to spare I started reading from my notes and when I got to the part about Miss Victory a superhero during WW2, the young man interrupted, "Contact the Comic Book Collectors Society, that's who you want to talk to. They have an office here in D.C." I heard a few tones and assumed he must have been transfering me but the phone went silent.. I looked at my watch and indeed, it was 5:01.

A Society of Comic Book Collectors? In Washington? I had no idea. Since it was past five, I thought I would have to continue this the next day. So, I turned once again to the 24/7 mighty computer. I typed in, Comic Book Collectors Society, and there they were—they have a page on Facebook. I have a profile so the link worked.

The society had a contact button at the top of their page, so I clicked on it and sent a message. They posted on their timeline that they also have a group so I clicked on that as well and joined. I took a couple pics, created a post and walked away feeling pretty good that I made progress considering I got up so late. Within minutes, there was a ding on my computer. It was a notification, and it was from the Society, a member commented on my post and so as they say, the rest is history!

Over the next few days of communications, commenting back and forth with members, an administrator chimed in who said he knew exactly who I was talking about and said he pinned my post to the featured section. This kept my post at the top of the group and soon after I found myself responding to a moderator who was also listed as an expert, Ms Marie Sovereign. She said she saw my pinned post and told me she felt goosebumps all over while looking at the pictures I posted.

A few minutes later, I received a private message via messenger. It was Ms Sovereign, who indicated it may be best at this time to keep a low profile. She confided in me that within the Society, there is a subcommittee—an elite group of scholarly individuals whose offices were downstairs from hers, some several floors below the society's office, literally, in the lower levels known as The L.O.O. or The League of Origins. A non-social media connected group of specialists whose mission is to document the origins and lives of superheroes, inclusive of all ages, especially those from the Golden Age, Including Miss Victory!

Ms. Sovereign seemed certain that the L.O.O. would most definitely have the information I was seeking and would be thrilled to receive an inquiry into what she described as the greatest age of them all, the Golden Age. She indicated that in her earlier days, during the end of the Silver and beginning of the Bronze Age, she was a librarian in the L.O.O. and did indeed hear of Miss Victory, but she had no specific information to share about her origin or whereabouts.

During our conversation, she mentioned that members of the league live their lives in the cool dry darkness, among the old paper they are sworn to protect, a low-profile quiet existence and informed me they can only be contacted through the old fashioned snail mail method, the United States Post Office. Marie explained, because unlike electronic communications, US MAIL leaves a paper trail.

She explained the procedure quite thoroughly, that letters of inquiry, which is what she said I needed to write, are scanned into the record by the secretary on receipt, and that the original is filed in the L.O.O. archives, a copy of which is sent to the clerk on duty for review. If the clerk feels your letter merits further attention, it shall be placed in the general mailbox to be copied and distributed to each member of the committee prior to their meeting on Tuesday. She informed me that the L.O.O. does not have a page or group similar to the C.B.C.S. but added some members of the comics society do intern at the L.O.O.. And the reason why she PM'd me. She wished not to compromise my submission mentioning I may have let the cat out of the bag by posting in the group. She explained that should the committee decide to share my inquiry with all its members, they will publish the letter on their private, members only website. Where it will be instantly accessible to the leagues entire community, domestic and abroad.

I was curious as to why the L.O.O did not have an above ground space and asked Marie if it was because the rent is lower underground, but Marie explained that was not the case at all — rather, the reason the L.O.O. is confined to the lower levels is because It's much easier and less expensive to control the temperature and humidity that is vital to the long-term storage of early, inexpensively mass produced acidic paper, namely pulp paper, which is what most Golden Age comic books are made of and printed on. During the 2nd World War, comics were not expected to last beyond the next paper drive and one of the reasons why many comics from that time are so coveted by collectors, especially those that survive in like new condition. As I was listening to Marie, I felt a great appreciation for the website I found where I saw and read the exploits of Miss V prior to, during and after the war, all at no cost.

Ms. Sovereign provided me with the address and suggested that I type, not write, for clarity, and sign my letter of inquiry, and mentioned it's probably best not to mention the suit at first, rather simply establish contact to get the ball rolling and hear what they have to say about Miss Victory. Needless to say, I did just as she suggested and composed a letter to the organization, inquiring as to what information the L.O.O. was willing to share regarding Miss Victory, such as where she came from and her current whereabouts, making sure not to mention the suit or the papers that emerged from it.

Chapter 2: A Gift from the Past

Several weeks later, seven to be exact, I received an old-fashioned snail mail reply from the League. Removing the letter from my mailbox and seeing the hand placed canceled out crooked stamp gave me the sensation that I was being communicated with by a real place with real people and not that of artificially generated intelligence.

> *Dear Stephen, Thank you for your interest in the history that took place during the golden age of comic books. The golden age of the comic book in America was and still is considered by comic historians to be the most significant age in the history and folklore of comic books. The golden age was not only the time when the superhero, as we know them still to this day, was born into existence, but it was also the time in history when America and the world needed superheroes the most. Not only did the superheroes battle evil head-on, but even more importantly, they inspired countless others to rise to the occasion and come together in an all-out team effort, stretching to all corners of the globe. Thankfully, they were successful in their efforts. Who knows if freedom would exist in the world today if not for the superheroes that emerged during the golden age.*
>
> *Because our files are limited insofar as Miss Victory's origin and whereabouts are concerned, the committee has communicated with all of its members in all continents regarding your inquiry, requesting any and all information regarding Miss Victory, from her earliest appearance and origin up to her current status. We are saddened to inform you that in both cases, we can share with you only minimal information when it comes to Miss V, none of which informs us of her origin, and also there appears to be no verified information as to her exit from the superhero scene. Miss Victory's file remains the same as it has been since the L.O.O. was created. No updates have been filed since. Our listing for Miss Victory remains the same - Origin unknown, current status unknown - rubber stamped, MIA. Missing in action. File - Open see comments.*
>
> *Members across our entire demographics appear to be very*

excited yet reserved in their response since becoming aware of your inquiry, which is quite puzzling since Miss Victory's file has been dormant for years. Several members have indicated they were under the impression you had information to share that surfaced most recently. This seems to have caused a considerable amount of speculation that is circulating within the league as to the existence and disappearance of one Miss Joan Wayne, who we know from Helnit documents submitted to the general files after the war, was allegedly known to be Miss Victory.

Please be aware that it is the League of Origin's and its members' sworn duty to locate, collect, study, preserve, conserve, and correct information on the exploits of all superheroes, dating as far back as June 1938 up to present times. Some members choose to go back even further.

There is a great debate within the league as to when the golden age ended and when the silver age began, but that does not concern Miss Victory, as she is not known to exist in the superhero universe after 1946, which many members have come to call the Atomic Age, and well before the Silver Age began at the onset of the second half of the 20th century, just beyond the initiation of the code of comics that formed in 1954.

It should be noted that there exists another woman superhero on record in modern times, that the league believes to have been inspired by and named after Miss Victory. Ms. Victory appears to be much younger and there is also a difference in the spelling of her name. We do not have her contact information at this time however we are 99.9% confident she is not one in the same as the Miss Victory in your inquiry and discussed here.

It has long been rumored that Miss Joan Wayne, aka Miss Victory, was captured by the Axis powers soon after the end of WWII and sent to Germany as a gift for Adolf Hitler, to be tortured, studied, and experimented on. There were also reports of Hitler's alleged demise in a bunker somewhere in Europe at about that time. Some members speculate that Miss Victory may have been at that location battling the Axis when the mountainside bunkers were bombed by the Allies. Many have assumed like so many others, Miss Victory may have been a victim of friendly fire therefore listed as missing in action.

There are other rumors that offer speculation that Miss Victory became pregnant during a mutually consented encounter with a black GI at the end of the war and that she has since gone into seclusion. This may hold water since there is a brief mention in the Captain Aero memoirs, which states: 'Miss V wants a family.' Several members suggest that this is pure propaganda from the Axis, created to distract from Miss Victory's capture, whereabouts, torture, and demise. This was known to be the Axis' method of operation, consisting of psychological warfare.

Verified sources at Continental Magazines document that the last known actions and whereabouts of Miss Victory is, that after a brief meeting with U.S. General Marlowe, an escort accompanied her to a nearby airport where she boarded her auto-seaplane and was spotted heading due east over the Atlantic Ocean, never to be seen or heard from again.

Otherwise, as it is written in her files, her origin and current whereabouts are unknown. In fact, her origin is completely nonexistent anywhere in comic book superhero history. To reiterate, all that is known of Miss Victory has been documented during the war by Frank Z. Termerson's Helnit Publications, Et-Es-Go and Continental Magazines. Sometime in 1944, the earliest missions were retold by Holyoke Publishing in an experimental one-shot format. All of these entities and their affiliates have long since become defunct. As originally reported by Charles Quinlin and Alberta Tews, and later by L.B. Cole & Nina Albright.

And let us not forget to mention the unknown, in this case unverified, among other contributors, Saul Rosen is suspected of reporting the very last known mission of Miss Victory in Captain Aero #26, published August 1946. There is still some debate over who is responsible regarding Miss Victory's last and final appearance. It should be understood that missions are not written, drawn and published until at least a month or more after the events occur.

A long-esteemed colleague of the LOO. Alex Kirby, a Golden Age specialist, wishes to inform you... and remind some of our colleagues, if they are not already aware.

In regard to the Golden Age, in addition to the known heroes who came to the world's defense during the Axis threat, there were many other unknown and undocumented heroes who took up the mantle of the superhero both on and off the battlefield whose stories and the documentation that supports their existence, have been either lost or destroyed due to the limitations in technology and the media that existed at that time.

Many technologies were not perfected, and the media used for documentation during those volatile war years were not stable and have deteriorated over time depending on the conditions in which they were stored, quite frankly, not made with longevity in mind. Most data formats that existed at that time were experimental, many utilized the cheapest materials, some designed to self-destruct after a specific amount of time once exposed to air. Microfiche used at that time was specifically designed for the war effort against the Axis powers of which employed extreme measures to prevent information from falling into the wrong hands.

We must be vigilant in our mission to preserve what we have left. As custodians of these artifacts, we have a responsibility to employ proper storage conditions including the use of acid free storage materials for our purpose and pledge as members to pass on our ephemera to future generations. Brittle documents cannot be made supple, but supple documents can become brittle, and this never ending deterioration has become our greatest foe. Once paper becomes brittle, there is little time left before it turns to dust. This is why storage conditions and materials used for rare and historical documents, particularly those made of pulp fiber, are of utmost importance without room for error. No compromise should be made. No expense should be spared.

In conclusion, as I believe all of our members are aware, there were thousands of men and women prior to, during, and after the war who carried out their missions in complete secrecy that did not live, did not survive long enough to tell their fate yet were victorious in their efforts. Sacrificing themselves for the future well being and safety of others, without reward or recognition. This was, still is and forever will be the cost of freedom.

The LOO would like to thank Alex for his insight. Indeed, it should be realized, understood, and remembered that many undocumented failures and successes have fallen into the realm of the unknown and unverified. However, we must never take the unknown and unverified efforts for granted or allow them to be forgotten. It is, in fact, the L.O.O.'s duty and mission to investigate, both individually and especially as a group, in an organized fashion to share and archive what we do know about those heroes and events as accurately as possible, even if there is little to no information available. There always exists the possibility that crucial information is yet to be discovered. Thus, all files must remain open.

The L.O.O. would like to take this opportunity to express gratitude toward Miss Victory and her many accomplishments. Because Miss Victory disappeared soon after the war, she may not be as well-remembered as she should be. She was not one of the more famous or powerful superheroes, but she was one of, if not the first, female patriotic superheroes to appear on the front lines before, during, and in this case, just after the end of the war. Miss Victory was highly intelligent, resourceful and extremely effective in her efforts. Perhaps even more significant was her influence as a leader in the concept of patriotism and loyalty to one's country, which is in itself a most powerful tool, especially when at war with such evil-minded foes, particularly those of the Nazi variety.

Miss Victory was unquestionably a genuine inspiration to those who followed in her footsteps, both female and male and those in between. She deserves to be kept in our fondest memories as a pioneer in the world of superheroes, for she broke the mold in a male dominated profession. Miss Victory appears to be the first real female of her kind.

That being said, we must also mention another female superhero, who carried the flag of the United States of America but disappeared just before the Axis powers engaged with the United States, known as U.S.A., the 'Spirit of Old Glory'. However, she did not appear to have a physical form. Due to this phenomenon, we must consider her a spirit, a ghost from a patriot's long past, perhaps even of supernatural nature, sent by God. There were reports in Quality Publications' FEATURE about her. For this reason, with an open mind, we must list Miss Victory as the very first patriotic superheroine in our records, in accordance with our current Overstreet guide.

Should you have any other questions or concerns regarding superhero patriots or any other superheroes, sidekicks, super vixens and villains during the previously mentioned ages, including the platinum, gold, silver, bronze, copper, diamond, current and future ages, please do not hesitate to write to this league's offices. We have enjoyed the discussion and awareness that your inquiry has brought to the attention of this league and its members. Regards, Max E. Newman, The Basement CBCS, attention the L.O.O. 101 Freedom Ave, Washington, DC. 10001

After hearing the league's response and the recognition given by the League of Origins' in appreciation for the significance of Ms. Victory and her impact on the United States of America and freedom-loving nations, I have come to the decision to donate the trunk and all its contents to the L.O.O.

Dear League of Origins, Please consider this trunk and all of its contents a gift to your esteemed organization. I believe this artifact rightfully belongs in your possession. Enclosed you will find a trunk dating from what appears to be from the 1950's. Inside the trunk, you will find what appears to be a hand made suit that I am certain you will find once belonging to the original Miss Victory, also known as Joan Wayne, as confirmed in the L.O.O. 's previous response to my initial inquiry, accompanied by a handwritten letter, allegedly composed by the owner of the trunk and all of its contents.

The suit appears to be, according to the letter, Miss Victory's very first outfit worn by Miss Victory in defense of her adopted homeland, the United States of America, and possibly other heroic patriotic minded efforts. I trust that the league will positively identify and verify the authenticity of this outfit and the holographic letter which fell from the suit's inside pocket during the initial inspection after discovery. Given the historical nature of this artifact and its significance to your organization, I believe this item in its entirety should be held, studied, preserved and displayed in the archive of the L.O.O..

Please note that I have included a second group of papers:

a translated into English copy for your convenience. I strongly believe that these papers, along with the artifacts so included, will prove convincing in furthering your investigations and should shed some light on Miss Victory's sudden disappearance after WWII. You will also hear Miss Victory share her secret origin. I suggest you sit down while you read the translation.

After careful study and consideration of the contents before you, it has become apparent to me that Miss Victory was aware of your organization and believe it was her intention that the League of Origins come into possession of these artifacts. I must warn you, to express the magnitude of what you are about to read, the letter of Miss Victory's own personal account, by her own hand, informs us who she was and how she came to be, and the reasons for her delay in sharing her story.

Please bear in mind, Miss Victory also explains at the onset that she has been diagnosed with dementia, a debilitating sickness that involves the degeneration of the mind for which to this day, is still without cure. Her origin is in my humble opinion not only truly inspirational but a most astonishing revelation, one that will not only reveal Miss Victory's surreal origin to the world but more importantly solidify her well deserved legacy.

I would like to express my sincere appreciation for your support and dedication to the memory of superheroes both known and unknown, documented and undocumented, from the past, present, and future. May God bless the United States of America, and all those who have done their part in upholding freedom.

Thank you once again for your commitment to preserving the legacy of the superheroes.

Part 2

Chapter 3: The Hidden Castle's Secrets

This is my origin. Miss Victory.

I have been informed by my doctor that my latest enemy's identity is known as Alzheimer's, a form of dementia. They used to call it getting old. She explained that my earliest memories will be far easier to remember than my more recent ones, which is a bit odd, isn't it? So, I will try to write this down as quickly as possible before my condition worsens. Please forgive me for any errors or omissions... and any confusion my illness may cause. I assure you, it's not intentional.

If you are in possession of this letter, then you must know about or have my very first suit as well. All of my suits are very sentimental. They each remind me of where I was and what I did in them. But the others are not as significant to me as this one. At first, I wanted my daughter to have it, but she said I should donate it to a museum. Imagine... (laughs) she's probably right. I thought I may one day send them the very last one. However, my daughter has already confiscated it for her own use. Not to mention, it is far more fashionable and much more comfortable because of the "V" stitched onto the chest, and of course, well, this is all I can say about that. I can tell you; she takes after her mother. Oh geez, maybe I shouldn't have said that.

What was I going to say? Oh yes, that's right. Well, I'm not quite sure where to start. Let's see, well, first I must tell you, like anyone who fights evil from within a costume, to experience any level of success, one must live in total secrecy. They must. Any other way would more likely than not spell death. Not to mention, you wouldn't get any sleep otherwise. In fact, my life was secret long before I chose to live my life in secrecy, and that may extend beyond my years, quite possibly long before I was even born. You see, I was part of an experiment born out of a test tube. Yes, it's true. Knowing what I know now, this is what I have come to believe. Today it wouldn't seem strange, but during the time I came to be, the thought alone was pure science fiction. The fact is, I have been, and still am, ashamed to admit why I disappeared so suddenly just after the war ended, that is, the 2nd World War.

First of all, I need to tell you, my name is not Joan Wayne. I not only longed to forget my past and who I am, who I was, but feared that should my story become known, I may put those I love most in grave danger. Not to mention, they would probably disown me if they ever found out... the truth.

Of course, now that my own time will soon come to an end... it does for everyone, you know, maybe one day that will change but for now, that's the way it is, so before it's too late, I want to tell you. I really need to tell everyone. I do. Let's see, oh yes, what I was going to say is... This is difficult for me, so please, please try to understand. In the end, I can only hope you can understand and that you will forgive me.

Okay, let me start this way... As a child, up until the day came when I learned otherwise, I experienced and knew only the good in my father. After all, I was a child once, we all were, you may still be, I know I still am at heart... I knew him as a good man, and so when I was young, I was quite fond of him. You could even say I was proud to be his daughter. It's very hard for me to admit, but it's true. Hmmm, I've certainly made a mess of this already haven't I?

When my father walked into a room, people stood up. They respected him. People did not sit until he sat, or he told them to. Right up until the time I was about to turn seventeen, I thought of my father as a great man. He was an award-winning author, a politician that was once loved by the people. He was very popular on the radio. Everyone tuned in when he spoke on air. I realize now, of course, that it was not love. He was a leader of men, and the men who followed him, followed without even the slightest hesitation. I can assure you, they jumped. Even when not in my father's presence, I was treated the very same as if he were standing next to me...

I didn't realize it at the time, but I had been born and raised in complete secrecy, hidden from the world. I never went anywhere. I was kept, kind of like a pet, but a prized example, similar to a thoroughbred racehorse.

I was raised on a very large, expansive mountainside estate, in a glorious castle built by a king. The best way to describe it would be to say it was nothing short of a fantasy land, very much like Walt Disney's castles in Florida and California, only with hills and cliffs, and enormous hidden caverns hidden by the enormous trees that surrounded them.

I was never bored. I was always kept busy, mostly with sport-like activities, building my strength and my endurance. And when I wasn't doing those types of things, I was also growing my brain, intellectually with regular studies... like science and mathematics, as well as art and music. These things kept me entertained but the emphasis was mostly on agility and strength. Which is what my father focused on most. I think it was his intention that I be born a male but sometimes you can't have everything. The fact I was a girl, perhaps he pushed harder. Of course, I loved my father, so I did everything he instructed me to do, and I tried very hard to excel without showing any fear, or lessened determination, which I learned only gained his favor. Daddy seemed very happy and very proud of me, that I was his daughter. But that's what I knew at that time. Everything seemed normal because it is what I have come to know as normal.

I was brought up not just by my parents, well, that's what I came to know them as, or those whom I assumed to be my parents, but world esteemed Nobel and Pulitzer Prize-winning scholars. I suppose I should be grateful that I exist at all. Nonetheless, my teachers were professors in all aspects of knowledge, including chemistry, mathematics, art, music, physics, literature, history, and even astrology. The stars were very important to my father, so they became most important to me. My father instilled in me that his goal was that I would one day win the gold. And so I thought, this must have been the reasoning behind my name and this motivated me to never give up.

Chess, the game of strategy, was also very important to my father, and I would play with my professors. Can you believe I once beat Albert Einstein at chess! My father didn't play, but he loved to have chess-themed get- togethers with his friends. My father would say to me jokingly, "If you are ever going to rule the world, my little Idola, then you must at least learn to communicate with the world. I want you to learn to speak Italiano, Englese, Espanol, Francais, Portuguese, Mandarin, Russian, and of course, Latin!" (laughs) I giggled and agreed, "Yes, father."

Father was a fanatical collector. He collected only the most valuable and rarest examples. Most of the things that surrounded me came not just from other collectors and museums but those discovered recently that shipped directly from the actual places where they were found. Many of which were once thought lost to the world, but he found them, or perhaps someone found them for him and he rewarded them in his own way. He was extremely demanding, and he had a very bad temper reacting to any level of failure. Men who made deliveries were sure not to slip and fall and break anything. Father would throw a fit if he found the smallest chip on the floor.

Many of the furnishings we had were not only original from when the house was built but gifts from other countries' diplomats, emperors, kings, and rulers from far-off lands. There were so many masterpieces in oils and golden artifacts that filled the walls of every room, originating from almost all places and times in world history. Even the hallways and bathrooms were overrun with world treasures. Like I said, my father was very fond of the things he collected.

His most favorite pieces were from space, including, as ridiculous as it may sound, an alien spaceship. It did not look anything like the spaceships we have come to know today through artist renditions, in fact when you first saw it, you would never think that's what it was. Not aerodynamic in the least. It was found buried in a tomb in Africa along with a golden ibis stick said to have once been used to rule ancient Egypt who at that time ruled over all civilization, previously lost for untold thousands of years until it surfaced and given as a gift to my father on his birthday. The most important pieces were kept in a massive vault far below ground, accessed only by a hidden elevator in the basement, a storage facility second only in size to the Vatican. The only entry was through a secret door in the study, one can only wonder how it was built.

He was completely infatuated with the rarest artifacts. He used to mumble while he napped that finding the Holy Grail or the Fountain of Youth would be the greatest gift he could give himself. (laughs) Imagine. Always for himself. I think he was really all he ever thought of. But what did I know? It was fun living in such a place with amazing and important objects.

This made learning seem a never boring enterprise, and it was a lot easier to understand and remember history and art when the actual artifacts you were learning about were at your fingertips. The love of history was something my father and I had in common. That is what he spoke about most... history and his place in it.

I did not attend outside schooling. I had what you could say was the ultimate in-home school education. In fact, I had never left the property for any reason until the day I left. We were isolated from the small village down the mountain, but I did have one friend who was my own age. Her name was Joan. The person whose name I later took for my own. She wasn't very strong, but she had a lot of spunk. And she loved to talk, which is why I loved her so much.

Every weekend, Joan would visit, and we would do all kinds of things. Since she had very limited physical ability, we used to have conversations about everything kids at that stage in one's life talk about. We played hide and seek in the garden's labyrinth, which was quite extensive. If you didn't know its secrets, you could be lost forever. We also made up our own games. Sometimes I would climb up a tree, and Joan would lie down on the grass below and order me where to maneuver about in the branches.

Sometimes the eurasian red squirrels would cackle at me. They make a cackling sound to warn outsiders not to trespass. We were never attacked more than a cackle. These squirrels are a bit different compared to the gray squirrels we have in the states. We had a lot of fun. Joan's parents worked for my father in the kitchen, making sausages on Saturdays and strudel on Sundays.

There were other boys and girls about the place, but they were servants and did not like to talk much. They were always tidying up, fixing curtains, lighting and extinguishing candles, wiping up dust that didn't exist, acting busy, while waiting for other orders. The other five days of the week when Joan wasn't around, I... as crazy as it sounds, I became friends with the objects and artifacts that filled the rooms and hallways. You were never alone, every bathroom had at least one bust of Caesar or other mythological God.

Yes, I talked to them. It was like there was a constant silent party going on in my head with all the works of art and worldly figures. Paintings by Monet, Picasso, Van Gogh, the busts of Plato, Da Vinci, Michelangelo, Raphael, and... anyone who was anybody was present, they were all there. I love classical music so I especially enjoyed fantasizing with the likes of Mozart and Beethoven. I found the musicians were the most pleasant, maybe because they were so handsome. I knew almost everything about them, and I could even hold a conversation in their native languages. The pianists seemed to have the most brains.

It's true, my imagination had developed well beyond most. This was actually part of my training since as long as I can remember, to hold a conversation with someone who is not there... talk about improvisation. The only time I didn't have to use my imagination was when I was with Joan.

I can't remember exactly when it was, but I think it was about that time when Einstein asked me if I played chess, which I did not and he asked if I would like to learn and of course I agreed. Before that he only made short conversation, hello how are you and goodbye. Every visit thereafter we played a game of chess. Early on the games were over quickly but as I got better, a single game could continue for weeks, which gave me time to consider my next move, until the day came when I finally beat him and we never played again. I think I was 13.

I remember once overhearing Einstein explain to my father that he was a scientist, not a magician, but he agreed to do his best to advance my maturity. How could you help but not laugh? I thought of him more as a comedian because he always made me laugh. So that always stuck in my head. His face would appear serious when he was trying to be funny and look funny when he was serious! I came to realize that this was the technique he used to increase my perception of reality. And so this is when I began to connect on a whole other level with the people and things that surrounded me. I came to know Albert more as a friend than as a teacher. I was just a kid eager to please. Perhaps this was the reason his visits lessened at that time.

Chapter 4: The Perfect Specimen

The doctors who checked on me were more like scientists than any doctor I have come to know later in life, they were more like inquisitive experimentalists, who gave me all types of vitamin boosters and enhancements. I think this may have provoked the situation I find myself in today. They either had success or failure. There were no in-betweens. Short term immunity is one thing, long term another.

I believe the reason I was never taught about medicine and the human body is because I might have been more inquisitive as to what they were giving me. I can only wonder now about the long-term effects of the medicines I was administered. I was given either a shot or a pill for pretty much everything I did including weekly injections, for reasons unknown to me. In fact I'm surprised I was fed real food and not a pill for meals.

I thought my mind and body were just fine at the time so didn't understand, nor did I question when I overheard them speak amongst themselves about brain enhancement through electric shock treatments administered along with specially formulated muscle-enhancing drugs, steroids as they came to be known, became part of the daily regimen. It seems quite clear to me now, that I was pretty much the equivalent of a lab rat, not a human being. At the time I thought my father wanted me to have all the advantages science and medicine had to offer, all the chances of success. For my success was his success, or was it his success that was also my success? I did not think much of the future, or the harm being done to my body. When I was young, as most kids do, I lived in the moment and considered myself lucky to have been loved so much. Ha!

Father always seemed to be coming and going. You found out when he was about to leave and when he was about to return when you heard and felt the rumble of engines and the footsteps of large groups of men approaching from nearly a mile down the mountain.

My mother always seemed to keep her distance whenever father was about to leave. Oh, I haven't even mentioned my mother yet, have I? I'm not really certain, but I'd like to believe she was my real mother, though I'm not sure in what capacity, if she was used to nurture me as an infant and later stayed on to give the impression I was the product of a natural birth and upbringing. Who would believe the child they came to know was born from a tube. I mentioned that already, didn't I? In fact I was never shown any photographs from when I was young, nor any other time in my life. Which is pretty odd now that I think about it. Anyways mom never went anywhere with my father rather she would disappear to her chamber whenever he was about to leave. I don't think my father wanted to take her with him either, so they both seemed mutually satisfied. In fact mother seemed relieved when he left.

This gave Mom plenty of time and the freedom to pray. Mom's specialty, when not praying, was dieting. She called it "fasting." It didn't make much sense to me at that time. I loved to eat. If I didn't eat, I felt like I would die. But now I understand. That's usually how it works in life. Some things just don't click until you have reached a certain point in your life. I wish I had gotten to know my mother better.

Mom made such a great effort to make sure that I didn't eat any of the most incredible candies and chocolates placed almost everywhere in the house. She said they were not put there for me, rather they were there for my father who was diabetic and had low sugar from time to time. Mother warned if I ate them, I would become a diabetic too. So she explained, it was a test of my will power. And I will be the first to admit, it was very tempting. But I refrained. My father explained it quite differently, that it was a good source of fast energy that is occasionally needed by the body. I realize now that my mother was telling me the truth and not making excuses like my father.

I can hear my mother right now reminding me, "The mind must always have victory over the body, so you must have a strong mind, not just a strong body. It is better that you have a strong mind and weak body than a weak mind and strong body. They both need cultivation." (laughs) I think my mother wished I was more like my friend Joan. Perhaps it was my mother who made my friendship with Joan possible.

I never realized by that time the reason why my mother seemed to have so much pity for me. She made me feel inferior, even though everyone else seemed to think I was superior. All the attention was always on me. We lived in that enormous mountainside monstrosity with what I thought was everything there was to have or needed to survive and be happy. Though, staying in that one place kept the rest of the world so much further away than it really was. But I didn't realize how big it really was at that time until much later in life. Seeing in books is one thing, going to a far off land is another.

As I grew into my teen years, I seemed to have developed this force around me, one of confidence and determination. I was very positive about my own abilities. I think what kept me from a completely domineering fantasy state was my mother. She was then what I would call today the only normal part of my life at that time. My mother and father seemed complete opposites. She was quite beautiful and my father. Well, I didn't think much of his attraction other than he was the one I needed to please more than my mother, yet I never saw very much intimacy on their part, but I never had that on my mind, so I wasn't aware of the signs, or aware of how parents act. The only other parents I knew were my friend Joans and I never got to know them. I was more of a tomboy. Now that I think of it, I don't think I saw any hugs and kisses or any other types of affection. Their relations weren't on my mind so much then as they are today.

When there were parties and elite guests roaming about looking at the fine art and artifacts, mostly on the weekends Joan and I were the only children at these types of events, but Joan was shy and didn't stick out, but she liked to watch me perform and was always there for me. She was my favorite audience. You see I was, along with my father, the center of attention until my father suggested that I retire to my room, which I couldn't wait for because on those Saturday nights, Joan was there with me and we had sleep-overs.

Once while changing into my pajamas, Joan took notice and asked if I was feeling well, she said I looked like I didn't eat. As far as physical status, I was developing into mostly all muscle, with negative 3% body fat. Not exactly healthy, but I assured her I felt just fine. I would tease her about my capabilities. That I was far more powerful than I might have shown her. I assured her my actions and reflexes were without the slightest hesitation and confided in her of my special treatment. We laughed when I explained how great it felt to take down men three times my size in one swoop. I explained that my father had plans for me to go for the gold in a future Olympics. I explained to her that running and boxing were popular sports throughout the world, especially in America, so they were extremely important to my father. Joan seemed to know this more than I thought she did. I loved to talk about these things with Joan, things that I couldn't talk about with anyone else. We would fall asleep fantasizing about the things we would do together once we were adults. The places we would go. The things we would see together.

I seemed to train as I slept. Dreaming of the time one teacher mentioned to another that I would learn more if I had only been beaten once in a while by those I trained with, but I never gave them a chance to lay a hand on me or take a full swing. I had learned not to give them any chance, or allow any leverage for them to strike back. Still, I was feeling great, not only powerful but empowered to a point where I felt no intimidation as I once did when I first started my training. It's amazing what you can do in your sleep. And now that my body had grown, I had much more of a snap in my step, with a certain lightness on my feet. And I can tell you, it did give me a bit of an attitude. So much so that I thought I could do almost anything. It seemed a step above mere confidence. What I came to realize as I grew wiser is not to show my confidence to anyone else, except of course my father. However, once confronted, in a hand to hand combat situation, It's wiser to act weak until the moment when you strike. The idea is to catch your opponent off guard. Afterall, I was just a girl.

The special drinks I was given throughout the day made it possible that I did not tire easily, nothing like those energy drinks they have today because whatever it was that I took helped my body recuperate at a far excelled rate. The status quo was to get a double day's workout in a single day. If I was feeling capable of more I took it to stage 3. That's 3 days. One time it was pushed to stage 4 and I passed out and woke up in my bed the next day. Did I mention I developed the ability to absorb high levels of energy on impact. I think this is where my mind helped the most, maybe through the electric shock treatments, insofar as my brain telling my body how not to react. Simultaneously calculating the force of impact and how best to shift, just inches one way or the other can make all the difference you know, by both lessening the impact and simply ignoring it, mentally speaking. As I grew to adult size, I seemed to develop very thick skin. Maybe the experimental concoctions were working, maybe they gave me an extra layer or two. Probably a combination of that and Einstein's calculus along with my fathers constant brainwashing were paying off. How this was to affect me later in life is something I wish not to talk about.

I never ever hesitated when my father gave instructions or failed to give the answer when he asked questions. By doing this I seemed normal, like I was doing what everyone else did, coming to attention and reacting on his order. Perhaps it was easier for me because he was my father, and I always did whatever he told me to do regardless. I made it a point to be the fastest in response. I wanted to prove to him that I could do everything he commanded and that I was the perfect daughter. I once heard him mumble to himself as he watched me while I was training. "I want perfection, I must have perfection, I must have a perfect specimen!" I wanted to be the very best specimen. I was indeed brainwashed, wasn't I? So every morning, with a fish-based breakfast, like a good girl, I took my vitamins. Vitamins with names like V-31, N-34, K-13, X-29. Sounds delightful doesn't it? (laughs)

When I hit maturity. I could do just as well, and in most cases, better than any man. I had developed skills that more than compensated for my smaller structure, in fact my size may have helped, insofar as gravity is concerned. I guess I had become my father's "perfect specimen!" He would call me throughout the day, and I would run from wherever I was like a gazelle when I received notice that he wanted to see me.

And he would squeeze my arms as if it were a drill, at least twice daily. "My little Idola, you are so special to me, my dear. I have big plans for you. One day, you shall see!" All I could think of was that he was planning to enter me into the Olympic Games in 1936, but he didn't, maybe it was because I was too young. He attended, I stayed home and trained. What were his plans, 1940?

I think I mentioned there were often parties attended by my father's higher society friends, oh yes, it was most humorous so I must tell you about it, he would call out my name in his own special way, "I-DO-LA!" Whenever he did this, I knew exactly what he wanted me to do. Perform on demand a pre planned choreographed display of excellence. I would, without hesitation, get to my starting point to establish eye contact with my father. Once made, on his nod, I would proceed to put my hands up into the air and perform a triple somersault through the crowd of guests who would need to move quickly out of the way while they were drinking wine and conversing on my way to the landing point adjacent to the seat of the Bosendorfer concert grand. At which point I would graciously sit down, take one deep breath, just one, there was no time for a second and perform "Flight of the Bumblebee" to perfection at a highly elevated speed! Within two minutes, it was all over, and the guests would shout with exuberance, and then the party resumed as it was. That's when I could freely breathe again.

I did end up getting really good at performing under pressure because of these playful acts. I practiced different routines many times a day, so I was always ready. And so, at these types of events, it became a regular thing. I actually looked forward to those moments and would be let down if it didn't happen.

I must say, everyone should learn to type, of course, in addition to having excellent penmanship. Typing was one of the most valuable skills I developed at a young age. There are times when it's best to write and there are times when it's best to type, each has a purpose. In fact I know there is a reason why I am writing this but can't think of it at this moment. As I got older and my fingers got bigger, I got better... and a lot faster. Typing seemed to come easy for me, perhaps because I practiced on that heavy-actioned grand piano for two hours a day. I have to admit, I found it very relaxing to go to the piano when my physical training ended. I guess you could say, it calmed my muscles so it was great therapy.

After practice, I would hit the books for about an hour or until it was time to eat dinner, after which I would head to the library where I would spend the rest of the day until retiring with a good book. Poe, Dickens, Hawthorne, there are so many, until it was time for bed.

Chapter 5: Unveiling Shadows

Everything seemed to be moving along quite well, and then one night, my life turned upside down. Or was it right side up? It was August 29, 1939. There had been some commotion regarding one of the guard dogs, Apollo, he escaped his kennel to chase after a rabbit when he apparently stumbled upon a dead body, buried in a shallow grave just beyond the target range in the most remote area of the estate, not very far from where Joan and I would hang out under our favorite tree. Wherever Apollo goes, his brother Zeus is certain to follow. They are very intelligent dogs trained to howl when something is foul. They must have known this person was dead or they probably would have licked him to death trying to revive the body. One of the men in black must have been there soon after to make the discovery.

That following Saturday, I expected to see Joan and wanted to mention this to her. She loved Apollo and Zeus and was great with all the dogs, but she didn't show up, and neither did her parents. This seemed odd to me. It hadn't happened for as long as I could remember, and the fact that strudels and sausage were so important to my father and his guests made it even stranger. So, I asked Emelie, one of the maid servants who takes care of the section of the house where I lived. She said Joan and her parents left unexpectedly in the middle of the night last Sunday and went back home. I said, "Home? But why did they not come today?" Emelie turned with a smile, "To their homeland, Poland!"

I was not only surprised but a bit angry. She left without saying a word about this. I got over it when I figured it wasn't her fault. Her parents probably didn't want to say anything to her because they knew she would tell me, which would cause me to ask my father and make it harder. So, I understood but was quite saddened by it. Joan was gone and I felt very alone.

Joan never mentioned she was from Poland. I thought her home was in the town at the bottom of the mountain, which I thought was where she was born. I never heard any mention of her being from Poland, though it makes a lot of sense why my father employed her father. Who better to make kielbasa than a chef from Poland?

I never visited her in the village down the mountain because my father said it was too risky, that I could be kidnapped and held for ransom, so it was not allowed. Yes, father did say on several occasions that I was one of his most valuable possessions and to never leave the specified boundaries for any reason. I accepted this fact knowing my father was a very important man and one way to hurt him would be to capture his only daughter.

That night, just after midnight, I went into my ninja mode and descended down to the kitchen for a glass of goat's milk. It was just then that I heard my father speaking hastily to a group of men in the study. I snooped close enough to hear what he was saying. "I told you to take away just the father, for interrogation. I didn't say to kill him and his family!" His man in black did not say a single word. Father then ordered that the man who didn't carry out his orders correctly be taken down the mountain and shot. And that the other man, or as he called him, the idiot who chose not to dig the hole deep enough, be taken away with the first man to suffer the same fate. The officer accepted the fate of his men without hesitation.

Wait! What man, what father is he talking about? What family? It can't be! It was at that moment that I realized the bodies that Apollo and Zeus dug up had to be those of my friend Joan and her parents. Did I really just hear what I thought I heard? Who else could they have been?

Needless to say, my head was spinning, and I felt sick all over. A wave of weakness came over me, and I managed to make it back up to my room without being noticed. When I got there, I realized I had forgotten the milk. Could it be true? Was my best friend dead? Was this really happening? I thought what kind of monster is my father? Was the man in my father's study really my father, or was he an imposter? How could he do such a thing? Why? Just earlier in the day, I loved my father with all my heart, and now, I hated him with all my heart and wanted him to die too!

I went to my room and stayed there. I think it was for the next two days. I shook and cried, trying not to, but I couldn't help it. I did not want to come out of my room for fear of seeing my father. I told Emelie to inform my mother that I felt sick and wanted to have my breakfast, lunch, and dinner in my room. It was the weekend, and there was nothing expected of me. This was the time when I usually spent my time with Joan, but now I was alone. I didn't tell Emelie what I overheard. I was hoping my mother would come to see me, but she never did. Did she even know what happened? If she did and knew I knew, maybe she understood how I felt but realized there was nothing she could do to change anything so didn't want to upset me any further.

While I remained in my room, my emotions were still in a state of shock, and I didn't want to leave and take a chance running into my father. If he wanted to speak to me, he would have to come to my room directly which he seldom did, at which time I would blame my sickness on something I ate. On day 2, it was sinking in and getting worse, Joan still had not shown up with her family. I lay in bed, thinking about my life, the past, things that now somehow seemed to make sense, at least more than they once did. Many questions came to me—questions about who I was, what my father's intentions were and what I was going to do knowing what I know now. I thought I knew my father better than anyone, but the fact is, I didn't know him at all.

Was I to remain my father's little Idola? I really didn't know how I could face him again. But if I didn't do as he said, maybe I too would be taken down the mountain and shot? Though at that point, I might not have minded, I would rather die than continue living with my father. But that finality didn't seem like the best decision. I must, in the very least try, try to avenge my best friend first. But how?

I wanted to escape, but where would I go? Where could I run to? How could I even get away? I didn't know what to do. The only person I felt I could trust to say anything to was my mother. Though I wasn't sure what she would have said, except maybe suggesting we pray. I thought of going to her, but I fell asleep.

I woke up abruptly the next morning, just before dawn, when I heard the rumble of a convoy approaching the mountain. Many men and machines were here to pick up my father. He left in haste without the usual goodbye, which worked out perfectly for me. Did he know that I knew about Joan? I was so relieved he left, and my headache subsided at that very thought.

All I had on my mind was Joan, so I ran to my mother at the far end of the castle to speak with her about what I had heard. But before I could say a word, my mother explained that Joan's father had learned of my father's intent to invade, destroy, and take over his homeland. He was caught sending a message to warn his family. Mother explained that the men were only supposed to take Joan's father away to be questioned, but apparently, Joan tried to stop them and was shoved away. She fell to the ground and hit her head on a rock, dying instantly. When her mother and father realized she was dead, they both broke out in a rage and attacked the men in black. They were both shot dead.

My mother said they couldn't have been taken down the mountain to be given a proper burial, because that would have disrupted the town's people. So my father decided to keep them here, and the people in the village would assume my father was keeping Joan's parents at the castle for his own use, sort of a reward for Joan's father's good work, all the while hiding any thought of what may have really happened, and the village people would be none the wiser. It's not like my father would have been questioned as to their whereabouts.

My mother said I should pray for my father. I wanted to kill him, not pray for him. I was confused about why she opted to pray for my father instead of thinking first to say a prayer for Joan and her mom and dad.

Mom said my pathetic father would not be back for quite some time. And while he was gone, there would be more people lurking about than ever, specifically, those dressed in black. Mother said I was to be aware at all times, warning me not to speak harshly towards my father because I might be heard. As much as it hurt to do so, I agreed to continue acting as my father's beloved Idola.

It's true, from that point on, they were constantly bringing documents to and from the castle. Whatever came in was brought into the office next to the study first until the documents were reviewed by the top brass, sorted, and eventually brought to one of the five underground storage bunkers on the grounds. As far as I know, there were five, I've been in at least three, I had no idea where the others lead to.

The men and women in black were almost everywhere you went, in the house and everywhere else on the property, some stationed far into the wooded areas. The grounds were flooded with men in black. I was not kept from walking into the wooded areas, but I was always followed and watched. They treated me respectfully at all times. The men would indicate to me that I was very beautiful and how great of a man my father was, and the women would say how they loved my father as if he were their father. As you can imagine, this was very difficult for me to stomach, and I wanted to throw up on everyone who said these things. I had fallen into an anorexic state; I just couldn't keep anything I consumed in my body. It all felt like poison. I needed to formulate a plan. What could I do to help those my father waged war against?

Now seemed like as good a time as any to use my mind as if I were behind enemy lines, what am I saying, I was. Physical strength was not going to solve this new problem. I did just as my mother suggested and made it a point not to talk ill of my father, even when I thought I was in private. My hatred was kept in my mind only, never expressing my true feelings with my lips, pen, or voice. These were self-thoughts only.

I kept a close eye, counting the number of boxes that came in and which bunker they went into. What were all these documents about? I had to find out. I had to act.

I could go anywhere I wanted on the property, and I never even tried once to leave, I wouldn't get that far anyway. No one ever questioned what I was doing when found looking through the files. After all, I was the direct descendant of the person whom they all seemed to work for and worship. I was showing an interest in my father's work.

I had become a spy in my own home. Eventually, I found out what I needed to know, and it was beyond belief. Apparently, my father had been planning this for years—to conquer the world! And to think I thought he was just being funny.

It was obvious that he had gone completely mad. In the more secret files marked "halt," I learned that he was essentially using Italy and Japan to his advantage. He regarded them both as idiots and fools, but at that time, he had no choice. He needed them, but what he did was convince them that they needed him. They must have been very weak-minded to have let my father lead them into war. They too must have been consumed by thoughts of superiority and world domination which obviously drove them to insanity.

Part 3

Chapter 6: Vanishing Currents

The files revealed so much, everything was laid out in plain ink. If Mussolini and the Emperor of Japan had only known the truth, my father would have planned to kill them both once he achieved his goals. Mussolini was to be fed at a feast and then drowned in wine. The emperor was to be poisoned by one of his close relatives turned traitor, whom my father promised a certain group of islands in the South Pacific. Can you believe it? Hawaii! This is why Hawaii was attacked by Japan when they entered the world conflict.

Armed with this information, I had to decide what to do. Sharing this knowledge would not have been only dangerous but futile. I did not want to make the same mistake as Joan's father. It was his mistake that may have actually saved my life. If I had not learned firsthand of his actions from my mother, the same fate may have awaited me. Sending a letter to someone warning of danger was not an option.

I tried to keep my composure and not go insane myself, focusing on staying busy and alert. I had become and was stronger, smarter, and far more aware of the situation that surrounded me. When my tyrant of a father finally noticed me upon his return on April 1st, 1941, over a year had passed or was it two. He smiled at me briefly before going about his business, which I now knew what his business was, he was more interested in his quest for world domination than in me. I of course smiled back.

When he saw me again later that day, he put on his fake fatherly face and opened his arms, calling me his "Idola." Oh, how I came to hate my own name. I was not an object in his museum, or was I just another idol? I hesitated just for a second as I started to run towards him, as he expected. I was saved from his clutches when a group of men dressed in black entered. He immediately turned away and went into the study. I followed cautiously to see what was going on.

As my father entered the room, the man quickly stood and made the Nazi salute, but wait, it wasn't a man—it was a highly decorated woman! My foolish father sat down, and all was quiet. He stared at the woman for nearly a minute before turning on a fan and directing it towards her. He examined her closely, asked her to turn slowly, and even had her let her hair down to create some kind of wild effect. The woman of course did as he asked before presenting him some documents she had obtained during her mission, emphasizing their importance.

Once the documents were in my father's hands, the woman proclaimed firmly, "PROPAGANDA, The AMERICANS!" My father nodded and commended the spy on her excellence, as well as her physical appearance. He thanked her for her loyalty, expressing his satisfaction with her performance and sent her off with the entourage she came with.

After everyone left, including my father and his aide, I went into the study, pretending to want to see him. There, on the Imperial dynasty table, I spotted the American propaganda left by the woman agent. I took the one on top and went back to my room to examine it.

It turned out to be a magazine full of color comics. I had seen comics before, but these were unlike any I had ever seen. The propaganda pamphlet depicted my father on the cover getting punched in the face by a Captain from America dressed in red, white, and blue, with a star on his chest, holding a shield that matched his clothing, it was quite marvelous.

Despite not knowing him personally, I couldn't help but find his actions endearing. Perhaps it was because I yearned to have the same courage, to stand up against my father and deliver a resounding blow. In that fleeting moment, I discovered a newfound affinity for the Americans. However, I knew all too well that entertaining such thoughts could lead to dire consequences. The very notion of liking the Americans was a dangerous admission that could cost me my life.

As I delved deeper into the story, a question nagged in my mind: How could the captain and his friend Bucky be aware of my father's plans all the way in America, especially when the country wasn't involved in the war at that time? Determined to find answers, I hurried downstairs and gathered the rest of the materials. As I voraciously consumed the tales, an indescribable transformation took place within me. It was as if a switch had been flipped, igniting a fire within my body and soul, something beyond anything I have ever felt. For the first time, I experienced a sense of connection and solidarity with the Americans, recognizing that, like me, they harbored a deep hatred for my father.

The following morning, as I returned the borrowed materials to their original location, I discovered a petite metal file box conveniently placed on an adjacent desk, bearing my name on its surface. With no one in sight, curiosity got the better of me, and I eagerly opened the box, extracting a substantial stack of papers. Intrigued, I retreated to the solace of my room to peruse their contents, only to uncover a startling revelation: these documents revealed the purpose that was intended for my life, and I found myself vehemently rejecting any involvement. Absolutely not! I refused to endorse my father's delusional ideas; I would rather die than comply. Could it be that this was the very essence of my existence?

There was no clear indication of the stage my father had reached in his pursuit of world domination, but it appeared that he was on the verge of involving me in his plans. I couldn't simply remain idle and await my fate. Was my sole purpose to be a pawn in his scheme?

I knew I had to take action, but the question remained: How? At times, I had contemplated taking my own life, especially when my father was absent. However, I always managed to convince myself that self-destruction was not the optimal solution. What purpose would it serve? It would render my life meaningless, nullifying all the training and preparation I had undergone.

I aspired to be a force for good, a valuable asset to humanity, rather than a burden. The idea crossed my mind—what if I could somehow attach a bomb to myself, one that I could activate with a hug as I embraced my pitiful father? But the question lingered: Where would I even acquire such a device? I could have probably manufactured one, I have the knowledge but simply assembling the parts required may be cause for alarm to those who were watching. Many hypothetical scenarios swirled in my thoughts. Among all the contemplation I had about ending my own life, this particular plan seemed worthwhile.

By sacrificing myself, I would have potentially saved countless lives. However, fear and uncertainty plagued me. The most rational choice before me was to find a way to escape that environment and seek refuge in America. Just the thought of joining in on the fight against my tyrannical and dictatorial father made me think more clearly and positively.

The very next morning, an idea sprang to life within me. Risky as it was, I knew I had to act swiftly. Time was of the essence. Faking my death seemed to be the optimal strategy, the only way to secure my escape. Naturally, for my plan to succeed, it was crucial that everyone believed my body was lost. Aware of the potential hindrance from my mother, I kept my intentions concealed, refraining from uttering a word.

To execute my impulsive scheme, I deliberately remained at the back of the training group that day. Dusk enveloped us as we approached the rope bridge on our route back to the fortress. Once all my companions had crossed the bridge and were ahead of me, I seized the moment and took a daring plunge into the turbulent rapids below. It was a now-or-never decision—a risk I had to embrace, prepared to face the consequences with unwavering resolve.

As I descended into the water, a shrieking noise escaped my lips, intended to draw the attention of those ahead of me, fostering the illusion of a slip and fall. Acquainted with the river's nuances from childhood swimming lessons, I possessed a precise understanding of where I needed to make contact. I navigated the waters with the knowledge of a spot, nestled between narrow rock formations, that boasted the necessary depth to shield me from striking my head on the rocky riverbed. Fortuity seemed to favor me on that fateful day. Reflecting upon the events now, I am inclined to believe that divine intervention manifested itself, as if God had dispatched his angels to protect me.

Aware of the likelihood that someone might spot me during their dash to investigate the commotion, I assumed a lifeless facade by floating face down. Holding my breath, I extended my arms, using my hands as a shield to safeguard my head from the encircling rocks. Carefully maneuvering my body around the obstacles, I proceeded downstream, sustained by my dwindling air supply. My objective was to convey the impression of a life extinguished. Just after the first bend, I surfaced, confirming my whereabouts, and promptly swam to a location where I could emerge from the frigid waters.

Having attained dry ground, I swiftly sought refuge within the encompassing trees, swiftly discovering a dirt path running alongside the river. Without hesitation, I altered my course, ascending the stream. Reasoning that anyone present that day and the subsequent search parties would likely concentrate their efforts downstream, I anticipated they would overlook the possibility of my escape upstream. After all, lifeless bodies do not typically travel against the current. An astute plan, wouldn't you agree?

As I make my way upstream, those searching for me downstream will be left empty-handed, their efforts seemingly in vain. With luck, the search will continue further downstream, towards the underground caverns and the pair of waterfalls that cascade into a purportedly bottomless lake. Recounted repeatedly during my earlier years as a deterrent from venturing into that region, it is unlikely that anyone would conceive the notion of searching upstream.

I'm glad I didn't inform my mother because it might have led my father to suspect her involvement in my escape attempt. She could have been thrown in where I intentionally fell, and I'm grateful that I learned to play chess.

A few thousand meters upstream, I stumbled upon a seemingly well-hidden cavern. I entered and found a spot to remove my clothing, allowing them to dry while I rested. I tried my best to stay awake, fearful that someone searching for me might discover me upon waking. If that were to happen, I would have to claim that I fell in, managed to escape the river, and was trying to find my way back home. Though I likely dozed off, I made a conscious effort to remain alert. Fortunately, I woke before dawn and resumed my cautious ascent up the mountain, keen on avoiding any encounters as anyone could potentially be searching for me.

As I pressed on with my journey, I couldn't help but contemplate the fate of those who may have faced extermination due to my sudden and unexpected demise. It was a price I had to bear in exchange for my freedom. My plan was to continue northwest through the Alps towards Switzerland. The distance wasn't extensive for me, and my prior training in this terrain was about to be put to the test. Adrenaline surged through my veins at the thought of being discovered, but once again, a stroke of luck or perhaps the prayers of my mother guided by God's watchful eye aided me. I stuck to the woods along the path, steering clear of any roads I encountered along the way.

Chapter 7: The Birth of Miss Victory

The following morning, I chanced upon a group of individuals engaged in a conversation about the change in weather. Recognizing the shift in language, I realized I had reached Switzerland. I emerged from hiding and approached these people, explaining that I had been held captive as a slave in a castle on the other side of the mountain and managed to escape by vanishing. I provided them with the name of my friend, Joan Wyspianski.

These individuals appeared deeply concerned and assumed a protective stance. They concealed me in a wagon filled with hay, transporting me to Swiss authorities. Shortly after, I found myself in the home of a Swiss citizen, where the authorities came to see me. I informed them of my desire to reach America and reunite with my family, who had left Poland just before the invasion. Without any hesitation, they embraced me, nourished me, and arranged for my journey on a train to Paris. Accompanied by a guide, I made contact with the French underground, and within hours, I found myself aboard a ship bound for England.

The presence of my father loomed over me as the sound of his aircraft filled the sky, accompanied by the reverberations of bombs dropping in London across the channel. It felt peculiar to be moving towards the sounds of destruction rather than away from them.

A group of women gathered together, offering their prayers, while silence enveloped everyone else. Evidently, these individuals had grown accustomed to such circumstances. Though everyone seemed aware of who was responsible, I couldn't help but wonder if my father had deduced my whereabouts and intentions, questioning whether it was me he sought to eliminate with his bombs.

Soon enough, I found myself in England without setting foot on land. I was directed onto a much larger ship docked beside the one I had arrived on. Given a loaf of bread and a cup of water, I was advised to be patient as I prepared to embark on my journey to America. The news filled me with excitement, and for the first time since parting ways with my friend Joan, a smile graced my face.

That night, I abruptly awoke to the sound of planes overhead as we sailed across the vast Atlantic. Instinctively, I sought cover, fearing the worst. However, a reassuring figure, who could have been my grandfather, gently grasped my arm and uttered, "Do not be afraid, those planes are friendly. They are the good guys." Glancing around, I noticed smiles of agreement and nodding heads in every direction. A voice rang out triumphantly, "The Americans!" and a cheer erupted among the crowd. The man leaned in and whispered, "We will be in America soon." Silence settled over us, and I soon drifted back to sleep.

As our ship entered the magnificent New York Harbor, I was roused from slumber by a young boy next to me. He was biting into a loaf of bread and excitedly pointing at the statue I had heard so much about during my train journey to Paris. Apparently my history books omitted this. But there it stood, a symbol of freedom—a woman holding a torch, a gift from France to America. It was an awe-inspiring sight to wake up to, one I shall never forget, the joyous atmosphere enveloping everyone around me was palpable.

The harbor teemed with an extraordinary vibrancy, a spectacle beyond anything I had ever witnessed before. It was almost magical. The air was filled with the distant melodies of music, echoing from every direction. Some of it was unlike anything I had heard before; I later discovered it was called Jazz—an exhilarating, liberating genre. I was about to embark on what had only existed in my books—the new world.

Once we arrived in New York City, we underwent quarantine, questioning, and were handed papers. We were instructed to keep these papers close and present them when asked, particularly for procuring food. These papers also served as identification, providing information about who I was and where I came from. It seemed to be the norm wherever we went, ensuring that others knew how to assist us. I had been assigned to a place called Brooklyn, where I received warm meals, clean clothing, a shower, and a safe place to sleep. The people I encountered along the way were remarkably kind, so I followed their guidance and instructions.

The food was different from what I was accustomed to—greasier but undeniably delicious. The sheer number of people surrounding me was overwhelming; individuals freely expressed themselves, unafraid to engage in conversation. In fact, I don't think I had ever interacted with people quite like them before that moment. This was a truly new and different world, and I found myself thoroughly captivated by it.

As I walked the bustling city streets, the crowd was dense, with people jostling each other in every direction. Occasionally, there were accidental collisions accompanied by a smile and an apology. These people's behavior diverged greatly from what I knew. For instance, one man leaned against a pole, casually smoking a tobacco stick. He flicked the ashes into the air and extinguished the glowing end with his foot, yet no one tackled him or made an arrest.

I distinctly recall passing a group of men observing the passersby. Their smiles were directed at me, and they tipped their hats, uttering greetings. One man even exclaimed, "Hello, doll!" and a couple of others whistled. Another woman explained to me the reason behind it, and I didn't mind.

Everyone appeared to be living in a state of happiness and harmony, as though part of one big, joyful family. Ah, yes! This was truly a land of dreams. No one raised their hands in exasperation, clicking their heels together. Instead, they waved their hands and called out names from afar, eagerly saying hello.
Such genuine friendliness towards fellow human beings was a novel experience for me.

As I strolled through the city streets, I noticed small structures resembling sheds on nearly every corner. These sheds housed racks upon racks of magazines and propaganda—similar to the kind my father's spy had brought to him. A young man stood outside one of the sheds, proclaiming, "Get your comics here! Only ten cents!" They were easily accessible, requiring only a small silver coin in exchange.

I really didn't even need to purchase the magazines; there were young people reading and sharing them with each other everywhere I went, it was only a matter of time before someone handed me one. Within these comics, I discovered stories featuring extraordinary individuals, predominantly men of great strength, intellect, and supernatural abilities. They battled the world's evils, including my father and his friends— Mussolini, Hirohito, and other deranged minds, often scientists who had gone astray. There were other topics, very funny pages, there was detective and mystery and science and so forth but I liked the ones with the Nazi's getting beaten up.

Gradually, I immersed myself in the lives of the superheroes and the prerequisites for becoming one. If that was the path I intended to follow, I realized that creating an alias or alternate identity would be my first step.

I had already adopted an alias, but I contemplated whether I needed an additional layer of secrecy. I pondered over what name I should choose for myself. It was essential to have a suit that would conceal my true identity and learn to act as two distinct individuals. Ultimately, I decided to change my last name, not my actual last name, but the one assigned to me on my papers when I arrived in America.

Responding to the name Joan came naturally to me; she had always been on my mind, my only true friend. So, I retained Joan as my first name, as it instinctively made me turn and look whenever I heard it.

Among the superheroes I read about, one stood out to me. He appeared more intelligent than the rest, and I admired his distinctive personality, he had style and a sense of purpose in life, not to mention the cave he worked out of below his estate, reminiscent of the one I had recently left, and as far as I could tell, he was single.

As an adult, my thoughts naturally turned to men more frequently than before I came to America. Perhaps it was because the men here were so different from those I had known before. Come to think of it, I couldn't recall a superhero I had read about who wasn't single. Many had girlfriends, but I couldn't find one who was married or in a committed relationship nor could I find a female superhero who was adorned in red, white and blue, the colors of my new flag. There were men but no women.

Regardless, thoughts of this one hero dressed in black, with a cape occupied my mind more often than I cared to admit. Nevertheless, given the turmoil engulfing the world, pursuing a romantic relationship was not a wise idea. It seemed more prudent to accept that I, too, could never be married. However, I allowed myself to indulge in fantasies of marriage and the dream of having my own family someday. I knew, of course, that it was purely a fantasy for the time being, and so, at that moment, I decided to take his name and become Miss Joan Wayne.

Changing my name was a simple process, many people during that time were altering their names to make them more readable and pronounceable. Filing the appropriate paperwork was all it took. I presented the document I had saved from when I first arrived in America. And thus, officially, I became Joan Wayne. Indeed, it was much easier for others to read, write, and pronounce than Joan

Wyspianski. I will never forget my dear friend's former last name, but it was time to move forward in order to fulfill my mission.

Once I made the change of name official, I set out to find employment—a job, a career! The prospect was exhilarating. I would be compensated for tasks that society expected of me—tasks that were both accepted and legal. It all seemed reasonable, even liberating.

In addition to my new name, I needed to devise a superhero alias befitting my role. Being a girl, which was not the norm in the comic books I had seen and read, I decided to use "Miss" as the first half of my new name since I wasn't aware of any other Misses at that time.

It seemed like the obvious choice and responding to "Miss" came naturally. But what should follow? It was in that moment that my mother's voice resurfaced in my mind, communicating a profound thought, what she had said to me so many times in the past—that the mind must achieve victory over the body. And so, it came to me at that moment: Miss Victory! My purpose was to triumph and bring down those who were in cahoots with my father, or any person or entity that threatened to dominate the world.

Thanks to my exceptional typing speed and language skills, I swiftly secured employment as a bilingual secretary at a well-respected law firm. My boss was deeply impressed by my efficiency, accuracy, and ability to communicate with anyone I encountered. As my worth became apparent, my rate of pay increased.

During the weeks I spent there, I learned a great deal. However, the job did not provide the leads I had hoped for in my pursuit of the bad guys. Nonetheless, it afforded me the time and compensation necessary to live on my own in secrecy while I crafted the superhero outfit befitting my mission—a suit that would, or so I believed, erase my past. I designed the suit as an homage to America's flag and the first American superhero I witnessed punching my father in the face.

Then, one Sunday morning, I stumbled upon the perfect career opportunity in the classifieds—a courtroom stenographer! This change in profession, although less financially rewarding, came with the fringe benefits I had been seeking. This new position granted me unlimited access to a variety of the files I needed to complete my missions. Computers had not been fully developed until after the war. How much time that would have saved.

Nevertheless, these resources provided leads related to criminal activities and background information on anyone who gave cause for investigation. Through the friends I've made in the system, I gained access to the most confidential insider type of information produced by government employees, including district attorneys and law enforcement officials. *In* a Federal position, I had access to the top-secret files held by the highest-ranking officials, including judges and politicians connected to various governmental departments on both state and federal levels.

Tax documents were also within my reach, and I utilized them solely to trace the flow of money. Whenever a high-ranking official received or made payments from dubious or illegitimate sources, it served as a red flag and a lead. My primary focus was on transactions that embodied an evil nature, hindering America's position as the leader of the free world. I had no interest in individuals or entities concealing funds from the government for legitimate purposes, such as buying a new home or car, as these actions ultimately contributed to the American economy. Instead, I directed my attention towards questionable transactions which in most cases were quite substantial.

Gradually, I developed an uncanny ability to detect the presence of malevolent forces, identifying inconsistencies within both the free market and the government through various transactions. Whenever irregularities hinted at corruption, red flags were raised, and I knew I was on the right track. This is where I wanted to dedicate my efforts, where I believed I could be a valuable asset to the United States of America, my father's most feared enemy, my new home.

Though I relished donning my suit and springing into action to defend America against evil powers that threatened democracy worldwide, I seldom found the need to assume my Miss Victory persona once I connected the dots on paper. However, nothing compared to the energy and thrill of wearing the suit and embodying American values and freedom.

Chapter 8: Reflections and Reunion

Towards the end of the war, the experimental concoctions administered earlier in life began to lose their efficacy. My body deteriorated as the effects wore off, and I came to accept that I no longer possessed the abilities I had possessed a mere 48 months before. Thankfully, this only affected my physical self, not my mind. Consequently, a time came when donning the Miss Victory suit was no longer possible. I suppose you could say that I carried out my missions from behind a desk.

There are moments when sentimentality washes over me, and I yearn for the feeling of putting on that suit and striking a blow against evil. After all, I am only human.

Months after I first graced the streets and war scenes worldwide as Miss Victory, I heard of a new heroine in town, a fellow government official. They called her Wonder Woman, a naturally strong, talented, and courageous young woman, described as an Amazonian beauty. I encountered her once in a secret military facility, but I did not disclose to her my true identity. However, I avidly followed her exploits through the countless stories I read. Truly, she lived up to her reputation. Undoubtedly, she will continue her superheroic endeavors for many years to come, far more visible to the world than I could ever hope to be. I am simply grateful to have been part of the battle between good and evil, standing firmly on the side of righteousness.

Just as my superheroine days were coming to an abrupt end, luck once again favored me. I was fortunate enough to meet and fall in love with a kind and affectionate veteran who had served as a medic on the front lines in the Marines.

We would have never met if Robert hadn't volunteered during his leave at the hospital where I received treatment after a close brush with death. We immediately connected, especially when he made me laugh by expressing his colorful opinions about my father. I found his humor both amusing and comforting. In fact, I didn't wait for him to propose; I asked him to marry me, and he joyfully accepted. Thus, I became Mrs. Robert Mar... Oops, I almost revealed it.

Oh, how I regret that I still cannot disclose my true identity, at least not my current one. Perhaps one day, it will be known. But for now, you know who I was long ago, in the beginning and I hope you can understand why I didn't share all of this sooner.

The one thing I cherished about Bobby was that he never probed into my past. He understood that if I wanted to share something, I would do so willingly. Well... I did mention it once, just before our 20th anniversary. I wondered aloud about my mother's fate in Liechtenstein, and to my surprise, Bobby arranged a surprise trip immediately after we boarded a bomber, which he called our "second honeymoon."

I had no idea where we were headed, but it didn't matter. I would go anywhere with my husband; he was my superhero! Bobby continued his service in the military and eventually became a top physician with the rank of Major General. We led a wonderful life, constantly traveling between top-secret military research facilities. I cannot disclose their locations; trust me, it's dangerous knowledge.

So, anyway... oh yes, upon reaching Zurich, I had to put on my sunglasses to hide my tears. Yet, I must admit, it was quite splendid. We stayed at a magnificent hotel with rooms reminiscent of my childhood bedroom when I lived with my mother. It evoked both bitter and sweet memories. It felt more like a reunion than a honeymoon, but it didn't matter. I was with Bobby, and we were free.

The next morning, we headed southeast towards the castle and made a few stops along the way to enjoy the sights. Each time I stepped out of the car, I discreetly put on my sunglasses, just to be cautious. I didn't want to take any unnecessary risks.

As we drew closer, a wave of goosebumps swept over my body, and my thoughts turned to my mother. She used to say that feeling goosebumps meant the Holy Spirit was present.

I had a strong desire to ask everyone I encountered about my mother, to see if they knew anything about her. However, I restrained myself and simply observed and wondered. If I had asked Bobby to investigate her whereabouts, it would have involved the CIA and other government agencies, and that was a risk I wasn't willing to take. He might have discovered everything about me, and I wanted to keep certain things hidden. Is that wrong of me? He despised my father so intensely, and I loved him for it. I'd like to believe he would have taken it as a joke and laughed it off. I suppose, at that point in my life, I still felt somewhat insecure about my past.

We eventually found the property, and as I gazed upon the remnants of the estate, which had been bombarded by the allies and reduced to rubble, I took a deep breath. It was a relief to see that nothing remained. I could only hope that my mother had escaped before it happened. So, I thought of her and said a prayer, hoping she had found peace wherever she may be.

Now, I look forward to the day when we will be reunited in heaven. I believe it's safe to say that while I will never have the chance to make my father suffer, he will surely face eternal damnation in hell. Bobby knows. I miss you, Muadda!

But on that day, I didn't have to utter a single word to Bobby. He could see it in my face and hear it in my heavy breathing. He knew that I had miraculously escaped the hell that he and so many others fought to save the world from—a war that claimed the lives of countless young individuals, all for the sake of a world free from such tyranny.

The price of freedom is incredibly high. I wish it weren't so, but that's the reality of life. When will we learn that there are better ways to coexist without ruling over others? As Captain Fearless once told me, evil will never cease to exist. Good cannot exist without the presence of evil. That's why superheroes and citizens around the world must rise to the occasion, understanding that evil is not the path to happiness. After all, everyone has the right to live a life of happiness.

My father undoubtedly deserved every profanity Bobby and others hurled at him, and then some. Just the notion of attempting to eradicate an entire race as if they had no right to exist is unimaginable and unforgivable. I now realize that praying for my father might not have been such a bad idea.

I am immensely grateful that I never succumbed to the thought of taking my own life. Just the mere contemplation weakens me. Please forgive me for being saddened by the fact that discussing my father is necessary to convey my past. My family knows nothing about him beyond what they have read and seen on TV, and unfortunately, it's all true, and likely much worse.

What I truly want to emphasize is that just because my father was evil, it does not mean that I am evil, nor are my children. You see, evil does not always perpetuate evil. I can only hope that my documented actions have proven this to you.

With love always,
Idola von Hitler

Acknowledgments:

I would like to express my heartfelt gratitude to Charles Quinlan and Alberta Tews, the brilliant artist and author creators of Miss Victory and their collaborators who brought forth the concept of Miss Victory at a crucial time when the world needed a female character to challenge the boundaries of women's rights within the predominantly male-dominated realm of the patriotic minded superheroes.

Coming Soon:

A series of stories that delves into the events preceding Idola's experimental birth, from the very idea of her existence through her childhood and development, chronicling the circumstances that shaped her design & purpose and even the possibility of other individuals sharing the name Idola.

www.ingramcontent.com/pod-product-compliance
Lightning Source LLC
LaVergne TN
LVHW012247070526
838201LV00091B/151

Future of Business and Finance

The Future of Business and Finance book series features professional works aimed at defining, describing and charting the future trends in these fields. The focus is mainly on strategic directions, technological advances, challenges and solutions which may affect the way we do business tomorrow, including the future of sustainability and governance practices. Mainly written by practitioners, consultants and academic thinkers, the books are intended to spark and inform further discussions and developments.

More information about this series at http://www.springer.com/series/16360

Vijaya Sunder M • L. S. Ganesh

Lean Six Sigma in Banking Services

Operational and Strategy Applications for Theory and Practice

Vijaya Sunder M
Operations Management
Indian School of Business
Hyderabad, Telangana, India

L. S. Ganesh
Department of Management Studies
Indian Institute of Technology Madras
Chennai, Tamil Nadu, India

ISSN 2662-2467　　　　　ISSN 2662-2475　(electronic)
Future of Business and Finance
ISBN 978-981-15-3819-3　　　ISBN 978-981-15-3820-9　(eBook)
https://doi.org/10.1007/978-981-15-3820-9

© Springer Nature Singapore Pte Ltd. 2020
This work is subject to copyright. All rights are reserved by the Publisher, whether the whole or part of the material is concerned, specifically the rights of translation, reprinting, reuse of illustrations, recitation, broadcasting, reproduction on microfilms or in any other physical way, and transmission or information storage and retrieval, electronic adaptation, computer software, or by similar or dissimilar methodology now known or hereafter developed.
The use of general descriptive names, registered names, trademarks, service marks, etc. in this publication does not imply, even in the absence of a specific statement, that such names are exempt from the relevant protective laws and regulations and therefore free for general use.
The publisher, the authors and the editors are safe to assume that the advice and information in this book are believed to be true and accurate at the date of publication. Neither the publisher nor the authors or the editors give a warranty, expressed or implied, with respect to the material contained herein or for any errors or omissions that may have been made. The publisher remains neutral with regard to jurisdictional claims in published maps and institutional affiliations.

This Springer imprint is published by the registered company Springer Nature Singapore Pte Ltd.
The registered company address is: 152 Beach Road, #21-01/04 Gateway East, Singapore 189721, Singapore

Dedicated to our families and friends

Foreword

I have been in the banking and financial services field for close to three decades now. During this period, I have witnessed the way in which the banks and financial organizations have evolved. The organizations have become more hybrid and complex, with a transformed focus on customer and cost. There is more emphasis on value proposition and the outcomes, thereby making data analysis-based decision making a way of working in organizations. Banks especially have become a competitive segment of the markets. In fact, the whole of services sector has been yearning not only to attract new customers but also to retain the existing, by providing quality services consistently, and the common problems include optimal utilization of the workforce within the budget crunches and to provide defect-free output to customers again and again. My favorite way of creating this competitive advantage is to deliver it through continuous process improvements.

I am delighted to write this Foreword, not only because Vijaya Sunder M has been my good friend for several years, but also that I believe in the practice of Lean Six Sigma. I also believe that Lean Six Sigma enables a unique combination of *speed* (of Lean) and *robustness* (of Six Sigma) in creating a quality management system that is required for today's competitive world. While Lean and Six Sigma have their roots from the manufacturing sector, Lean Six Sigma has worked really well in the context of service quality, especially in banking and financial services. But, to the best of my knowledge, there are not many books specific to banking on this subject.

In the beginning, this book establishes a systematic way to identify research gaps in the body of knowledge of Lean Six Sigma across services, using morphological analysis, a systems thinking technique. Then, it establishes how Lean Six Sigma could lead an organization toward gaining higher stakeholders' satisfaction. The authors establish this through three interesting real-time cases of Lean Six Sigma project management from global banks and subsequently discussing the managerial implications. The cases include (1) optimizing employee utilization in a bank, (2) rejects reduction in accounts opening of a bank's back office, and (3) improving accuracy in payments processing. Making you believe and reaffirm these operational benefits that Lean Six Sigma projects would deliver, authors then question you—is that all Lean Six Sigma has to offer?

Then, the book takes on longitudinal case-evidence to present a novel, strategic view of Lean Six Sigma toward creating a competitive advantage in quality. You will find a strategic orientation of Lean Six Sigma beyond its operational benefits. Alongside the real-time Lean Six Sigma project management cases in the banking context, this book offers a fresh dynamic capabilities perspective. The authors argue that when looked through the dynamic capabilities lens, Lean Six Sigma offers a platform to create a competitive advantage in quality. Reading this book, you will find it hard to defend Lean Six Sigma as merely a continuous improvement practice that could be deployed through executing a few projects. The book provides a compelling strategic view that a core quality management practice can be a higher-order capability in organizations.

Another interesting feature of this book is its presentation and flow of contents that anyone who does not even know much about quality management can easily understand and enjoy reading it. In the first two chapters, the authors set a background by introducing the key concepts in a way that even if the reader does not have any pre-requisite knowledge about quality management, should be able to understand the rest of the contents of the book easily.

This book caters to the needs of both researchers and managers by contributing to both theory and practice. I hope this book will become a primer among quality management researchers, operations strategy managers, and continuous improvement practitioners, as it triggers applied thought leadership in operational excellence in the context of banking and beyond.

Mumbai, India

Kunda Jadhav
Director and Head—India Operations
Scotiabank

Acknowledgements

Prima facie, we are grateful to the Almighty God. In the interesting journey that this book has been through, we received help, support, advice, and guidance from several people. First and foremost, we would like to thank the publisher of this book—Springer Nature Singapore—and a number of colleagues in industry for their constant encouragement in writing up this book. We are thankful to Prof. David Teece (Haas School of Business, University of California, Berkeley), Prof. Jiju Antony (Heriot-Watt University), and Prof. Rahul R. Marathe (IIT Madras) for their comments that have added value to this book. We are thankful to Emerald Publishing Limited and Taylor & Francis Group for providing us permissions to use some of our published work[1] in their journals as part of this book. We would like to express our deepest appreciation to Nupoor Singh in Springer Nature for her support and forbearance during the course of the project. Finally, we would like to express our sincere thanks to our parents and family as the book stole significant hours away from family activities. Last but not least, we are thankful to all our colleagues and friends for their love and support.

Vijaya Sunder M
L. S. Ganesh

---

[1]DOIs: 10.1080/09537287.2016.1187312, 10.1108/IJOPM-05-2016-0273, 10.1108/ijqrm-01-2019-0012.

Praise for *Lean Six Sigma in Banking Services*

"This book provides a deep understanding of Lean Six Sigma applications. It inspires by transferring the principles of the concept into uncommon areas of operations and management behind the usual quality and project management. While reading the book I got hit by a great idea of applying Lean Six Sigma in my digital business as well. My impression at the end of the book was that sky is the limit for the right employment of Lean Six Sigma, especially while viewing it from a dynamic capabilities' lens. Readers of this book will surely receive insights for improving their business processes both operationally and strategically. Although the book is focused on banking, it is actually suitable for a really wide audience. This is a brilliant piece of research as a book that will serve as a guide for transformation by the prism of Lean Six Sigma."
 —Professor Dr. Zornitsa Yordanova, *Chief Assistant Professor of Innovation Management, University of National and World Economy, Sofia, Bulgaria*

"Lean Six Sigma needs to be understood from a systems perspective and there exists a huge knowledge gap in this area of finding holistic solutions to business problems. This book is a very welcome work that addresses this call. It integrates quality management resources and dynamic capabilities view towards practice. Banking and Financial Services was aptly chosen as it has the most direct applicability for social enterprises. Anyone interested in creating more impact with less will surely benefit from reading the book."
 —Alex Abraham, *Chief Executive Officer, Lean Success Partners, Winnipeg, Manitoba, Canada*

"The book is a refreshing booster to the world of Quality Management especially in the context of Banking and Financial Services. Concepts and terms like 'Rapidness of Lean & robustness of Six Sigma to solve operational problems' 'Hybrid methodology' resonate very well with what we do in the industry today. Another interesting fact about the book is applying 'Dynamic Capabilities approach' to Quality Management, that sets a fresh Quality Oven and ensures this book is definitely a good investment of authors' intellect. Best part—Even if a reader is new to the world of Quality, this book will be appropriate and resonating. For

Researchers and Practitioners, both being leaders or fresh entrants, this book stands out to be a must-read, as it demonstrates the success of the Lean Six Sigma methodology via case studies and practical applications."
—Udit Salvan, *Director, Global Transformation & Engineering Network, An American Multinational Financial Services Corporation, New York, USA*

Contents

1 **Introduction** 1
   1.1   Continuous Improvement Through Lean and Six Sigma 3
   1.2   From Lean and Six Sigma to Lean Six Sigma 4
   1.3   Purpose and Scope of This Book 5
   1.4   What Can You Expect from This Book? 7
   References 9

2 **Background of Key Concepts** 11
   2.1   A Brief Overview of Service Quality 12
   2.2   Continuous Improvement 13
   2.3   Organizational Learning in the Context of CI 14
   2.4   Lean Services—Successes and Shortcomings 15
   2.5   Six Sigma in Services—Successes and Shortcomings 16
   2.6   A Brief Overview of Lean Six Sigma 18
   References 20

3 **An Overview of Banking Sector** 23
   3.1   An Overview of Global Banking Picture 24
   3.2   An Overview of LSS in Banking 25
   3.3   Understanding Key Performance Indicators in Banks
         for Deriving LSS Opportunities 26
   References 27

4 **Lean Six Sigma for Services—A Morphological Analysis
of Research Literature** 29
   4.1   An Overview of Lean Six Sigma in Services 29
   4.2   Data from Literature and Their Classification 30
         4.2.1   Fundamental Classification of LSS Research 31
         4.2.2   Methodological Classification of LSS Research 31
         4.2.3   Chronological Classification of LSS Research 32
         4.2.4   Sector-Wise Classification of LSS Research 34
   4.3   Morphological Analysis of the Literature 35
         4.3.1   Dimension 1: Organizational Context of Application 35
         4.3.2   Dimension 2: Desired Outcomes 36

		4.3.3	Dimension 3: Implementation Systems	37
		4.3.4	Dimension 4: LSS Tools and Techniques	38
		4.3.5	Dimension 5: Integration with Other Philosophies	38
		4.3.6	Dimension 6: Evaluation Methods	38
	4.4	Discussion		39
	References			41
5	**Lean Six Sigma Projects in Banking Firms—Implementation Cases**			43
	5.1	An Overview of Research Literature on LSS in Banking		43
	5.2	Evidence from Practitioners' Literature		44
	5.3	Real-Time Applications of LSS in Banking		44
		5.3.1	Approach to LSS Project Management	45
		5.3.2	LSS Project Management Method Used	46
	5.4	Case Studies		47
		5.4.1	Case A: Optimization of Employee Utilization	47
		5.4.2	Case B: Rejects Reduction in Accounts Opening of a Bank's Back Office	54
		5.4.3	Case C: Accuracy Improvement in Payments Processing	63
	5.5	Lessons Learned and Managerial Implications		69
		5.5.1	LSS as a Systems Approach for Process Improvement	69
		5.5.2	Identification of Correct LSS Candidates	70
		5.5.3	LSS Project Management Is a Subset of LSS Deployment	70
		5.5.4	Management of Stakeholders in LSS Projects	71
		5.5.5	Change Leadership for LSS Projects	71
	5.6	Summary of This Chapter		72
	References			72
6	**Lean Six Sigma as a Dynamic Capability in Banking Firms**			75
	6.1	Organizational Capabilities		75
	6.2	Dynamic Capabilities		77
	6.3	Approach to Study the Strategic Orientations		79
	6.4	Findings from a Dynamic Capabilities' Perspective		83
		6.4.1	Compelling Need for Purposive Creation of LSS Capability	83
		6.4.2	LSS as a Vital Component of the Capabilities Network	83
		6.4.3	Path Dependency and Emergence	84
		6.4.4	LSS Enables Organizational Learning	84
		6.4.5	Technical and Evolutionary Fitness of LSS	85
		6.4.6	LSS Exhibits VRIN Characteristics	87
		6.4.7	LSS Exhibits Agility Towards Environmental Dynamism	88

	6.5 Summary of This Chapter	89
	References	90
7	**Summary and Conclusions**	93
	Reference	95

About the Authors

Dr. Vijaya Sunder M is an Assistant Professor, Operations Management at Indian School of Business (ISB), Hyderabad, India. In the past, he was the Head of Business Process Excellence at the World Bank Group. Vijaya holds a PhD in Operational Excellence from Indian Institute of Technology (IIT) Madras, a distinction in Master of Business Administration from the Sri Sathya Sai Institute of Higher Learning, and a gold medal in Bachelor of Engineering from the Anna University, India. He is a Lean Six Sigma Master Black Belt, ISO 9001:2015 Quality Lead Auditor, and Lean Facilitator. He has led and mentored various re-engineering and process improvement programs that helped improve the customer experience, employee satisfaction, eliminate process defects, increase productivity and reduce costs across reputed organizations including the World Bank, Barclays, American Express and Citi Group. His research and teaching interests include Operational Excellence, Project Management, Quality Management, Industry 4.0 and Operations Strategy. He has published research papers on quality management and operational excellence in several respected international journals.

Dr. L. S. Ganesh is a Professor in the Department of Management Studies at the Indian Institute of Technology (IIT) Madras, India. Ganesh holds a Bachelor of Engineering (Hons.) degree in Mechanical Engineering from BITS Pilani, and an MTech in Maintenance Engineering and Management from IIT Madras. He completed his PhD from IIT Madras with a thesis on educational planning in Tamil Nadu schools. From then on, he has held many responsible positions including, being the Head of the Department and Dean (Students) at IIT Madras. He is a Distinguished Fellow of the Project Management Institute (India). His research and teaching interests span a wide range of areas including Systems Thinking, Project Management, Knowledge Management, Public Systems (Education and Energy) and Entrepreneurship.

Abbreviations

ABS	Association of Business Schools
BFS	Banking and Financial Services
CI	Continuous Improvement
CMMI	Capability Maturity Model Integration
COPC	Customer Operations Performance Centre
CTQ	Critical to Quality
DC	Dynamic Capability
DMADOV	Define-Measure-Analyze-Design-Optimize-Verify
DMADV	Define-Measure-Analyze-Design-Verify
DMAIC	Define-Measure-Analyze-Improve-Control
DPMO	Defects per Million Opportunities
FMEA	Failure Modes Effects Analysis
FTE	Full Time Employee
GDP	Gross Domestic Product
ISO	International Organization for Standardization
IT	Information Technology
ITES	Information Technology Enabled Services
JIT	Just-In-Time
KPI	Key Performance Indicator
LSS	Lean Six Sigma
MA	Morphological Analysis
OCs	Operational Capability
OM	Operations Management
PDCA	Plan-Do-Check-Act
PI	Process Improvement
PPM	Parts Per Million
PRA	Probabilistic Risk Assessment
QFD	Quality Function Deployment
R&D	Research and Development
RBV	Resource Based View
SERVPERF	Service Performance
SERVQUAL	Service Quality
ST	Systems Thinking
TPM	Total Preventive Maintenance

TPS	Toyota Production Systems
TQM	Total Quality Management
VOC	Voice of the Customer
VRIN	Valuable- Rare- Inimitable- Non-Substitutable

List of Figures

Fig. 1.1	Funnel diagram to illustrate the scope	6
Fig. 1.2	Concept map showing the linkages of chapters of this book	8
Fig. 4.1	Concept map of this chapter	30
Fig. 4.2	Concurrent research analysis matrix	40
Fig. 5.1	Project charter	48
Fig. 5.2	Process capability of the baseline data	49
Fig. 5.3	Fishbone diagram of high employee utilization	50
Fig. 5.4	Process capability post-improvements	54
Fig. 5.5	Swimlane process map	56
Fig. 5.6	Measurement system analysis	57
Fig. 5.7	Process capability (before project)	58
Fig. 5.8	Cause–effect diagram	59
Fig. 5.9	Process capability (after project)	63
Fig. 5.10	5-Why analysis	66
Fig. 5.11	Defect rate—before versus after LSS project	68

List of Tables

Table 2.1	DMAIC common tools	20
Table 4.1	Methodological classification of reviewed papers	32
Table 5.1	Data and process analysis	51
Table 5.2	Project charter	55
Table 5.3	Causes of the problem	60
Table 5.4	Improvement plan	62
Table 5.5	Summary of the project charter	64
Table 5.6	Process capability with baseline data	65
Table 5.7	Pareto analysis	65
Table 5.8	Process capability post-improvement	68
Table 5.9	Project selection criteria	70
Table 6.1	Summary of interviews	81

Introduction 1

In today's competitive world, organizations compete with each other not only to attract customers but to retain them by providing consistent quality of goods and services on time and every time. History shows instances of how industries have transformed over time, and every time a revolution has taken place, there have been new ways of working using newer technologies. The beginning of the twentieth century saw the development of a number of management programs that made it possible to increase the efficiency and effectiveness of manufacturing facilities. Mass production of goods using assembly lines became commonplace. The last few decades of the twentieth century witnessed integrated systems, customized products and services, and formalization of the supply chain management concept. Pressure to reduce costs caused many firms to move their operations to low-cost countries. But things have changed in the twenty-first century. Industry 4.0 opens opportunities to connect technologies to guide operations for developing new ways of working. At this juncture, erstwhile quality management strategies like Lean may not completely fulfill the purpose. Different industries have evolved their own ways of working by applying the contemporary Lean Six Sigma method, which has gained attention in the past few years. Being a hybrid methodology that integrates and synergizes Lean principles with the Six Sigma toolkit, Lean Six Sigma enables a unique combination of speed and robustness in manufacturing and services. While quality management practices including Lean Six Sigma fall under the operations management discipline, their applications are truly multi-disciplinary, with an ultimate aim to create competitive advantage for organizations.

"Competitive advantage" is among the most widely used terms in the field of strategic management. Despite the differences between a monopolistically competitive market and a perfectly competitive market, every firm works to maximize its profitability and market presence. In a generic sense, an organization's competitive advantage is the primary attribute that enables it to outperform its competitors. Encapsulating the understanding from the earliest works such as Schumpeterian theories of innovation-based competition among organizations and the later strategic management theories of competitive advantage such as the competitive forces approach (Porter 1985), the core competencies approach (Prahlad and Hamel 1990) and the resource-based approach (Barney 1991; Makadok 2001), the dynamic capabilities approach (DCA) has evolved into a distinct body of knowledge for scholarly research since its origins in the 1990s. The founding thinkers (Teece et al. 1997) defined DCA as a firm's ability to alter its resource configurations through applying certain capabilities and thus adapt to changing environments to achieve new forms of competitive advantage. Amidst the loops of criticisms and defenses, the DCA has attracted substantial attention from scholars publishing in top-tier management journals. According to a study, more than 1500 published articles appeared in the ABI/INFORMS database between 1997 and 2007 on DCA (Barreto 2010) and this count has significantly increased even recently (Schilke et al. 2018). To develop competitive advantage in quality, it is essential that organizations realize the big picture of a firm not restricting quality management to operations alone. The essential interface of operations management and strategy, known to be as "operations strategy," is essential for this effect.

Operations strategy scholars often use high quality performance relative to competition as an indicator of a competitive advantage with reference to quality (Ward and Duray 2000). Competitive advantage based on quality is an ability of a firm to achieve a high level of quality performance at a point in time and do it consistently over time (Hannan and Freeman 1984; Su et al. 2014). Earlier, researchers have drawn on different theoretical perspectives to understand the relationship between quality and competitive advantage. For example, scholars have drawn on the resource-based approach (Barney 1991) of the firm to explain how several practices and frameworks such as total quality Management (Flynn et al. 1994; Powell 1995), the Malcom Baldrige Business Excellence evaluation framework (Flynn and Saladin 2001), and the ISO 9000 Quality Management System (Martínez-Costa et al. 2009) lead to competitive advantage in quality. However, very little has been studied about how to sustain competitive advantage in quality (Su et al. 2014).

While high quality performance could lead to competitive advantage, what matters is a firm's ability to create that "capability." Due to the growing pace and complexity of business environments, organizations no longer compete on processes but on their ability to continually improve processes (Teece 2007), and this phenomenon is called as "continuous improvement." A few practices to effect continuous improvement have been observed to exhibit some characteristics beyond operational capabilities (Anand et al. 2009; Benner and Tushman 2003; Zollo and Winter 2002) and have been candidates to be considered as DCs. Although operations management scholars and executives realize the importance of continually improving processes, their efforts have been predominantly focused on building process efficiencies for operational benefits like cost reduction, resource optimization, defect reduction. This leaves an opportunity to investigate the strategic outcomes of continuous process improvement initiatives, toward deriving a competitive advantage with reference to quality in firms.

The common aim of continuous improvement programs is to provide standardized mechanisms for continuous process changes across different functions of the firm, and with alliance partners, suppliers, and customers. Among several other continuous improvement initiatives, Lean and Six Sigma are regarded among the most popular contemporary management strategies used in organizations (Albliwi et al. 2014). Though Lean and Six Sigma were developed independently, both these powerful continuous improvement strategies have emerged from Japanese ways of working, adapted across the globe.

1.1 Continuous Improvement Through Lean and Six Sigma

The common aim of continuous improvement programs is to provide standardized mechanisms for continuous process changes across different functions of the firm, and with alliance partners, suppliers, and customers. Among several other continuous improvement initiatives, Lean and Six Sigma are regarded among the most popular contemporary management strategies used in organizations (Sunder M and Prashar 2020). Though Lean and Six Sigma were developed independently, both these powerful continuous improvement strategies have emerged from Japanese ways of working, adapted across the globe.

Lean is a continuous improvement methodology that focuses on reducing cycle time and waste in the processes. James P. Womack and Daniel T. Jones coined the term "Lean Thinking" in 1996 (Womack and Jones 1997). Lean is a systematic approach to identify and eliminate waste through continuous improvement; flowing the product at the pull of the customer in pursuit of perfection. The expanded application of Lean practices in recent years across the world has been popularized from manufacturing to transactional and service industries. According to Stewart and Meyers (2002), waste is defined as anything that does not add value to the end-product from the consumer's perspective. According to Lean methodology, waste can be of seven categories: overproduction, inventory, over-processing, motion, waiting, defects, and transportation (Rawabdeh 2005). Lean organizations are capable of producing high-quality products economically in lower volumes and bringing them to markets faster than mass producers. A Lean organization can make twice as much of a product with twice the quality and half the time and space, at half the cost, with a fraction of the normal work-in-process inventory (Sharma 2014). Lean management is about operating the most efficient and effective organization possible, with least cost and zero waste. According to the Lean approach, the value of a product is defined solely based on what actually the customer requires and is willing to pay for. All activities can be grouped into three types:

(a) value-added activities: these are activities that transform the inputs into the exact product or service that the customer requires;
(b) necessary, but non-value-added activities: these are activities that do not add value from the perspective of the customer, but are necessary to deliver the product or service, unless the existing supply or process is radically changed; and

(c) non-value-added activities: these are activities which are not required for transforming the materials into the product or service that the customer wants, and must hence be eliminated or avoided.

5S, value-stream mapping, JIT, poka-yoke, and visual controls are a few of the Lean techniques which organizations follow to deploy Lean. Chrysler used resources to extend in-house training of Lean philosophy to its major suppliers, emphasizing the commitment needed from all parties to establish Lean, and realize the full potential for everyone involved (Fitzgerald 1997). Delphi and Mitsubishi are a few other organizations that have benefited from Lean.

Six Sigma, initially developed at Motorola in the 1970s, was a business transformation initiative based on effecting breakthroughs in quality enhancement. Motorola initiated the Six Sigma program focusing on their customer requirements to produce defect-free outputs. Later in 1988, Motorola won the Malcom Baldrige Quality Award and outperformed their competitors with its use of Six Sigma, which has often been presented as something different from TQM. Six Sigma is so different from other quality initiatives because it makes organizations make more money by improving customer value and efficiency, with the benefits going straight to the bottom line (Pyzdek 2003). Motorola saved $15 billion during 11 years of adopting their Six Sigma discipline. Following Motorola, many organizations across different markets realized the importance of this unique technique and gained competitive advantage. For example, General Electric gained more than $2 billion as customer benefits in 1999, because of their Six Sigma efforts (Lucas 2002). Allied Signal had productivity gains of 6% in manufacturing in a two-year period. Gerald Defoe, a quality engineer in the New York Air Brake Company, noted that Six Sigma put the whole problem-solving process into a very structured format (DeFeo 2000). DMAIC (Define-Measure-Analyze-Improve-Control) is the most commonly used roadmap by organizations for continuous improvements. Define-Measure-Analyze-Design-Validate (DMADV) and Define-Measure-Analyze-Design-Optimize-Validate (DMADOV) are a few other Six Sigma roadmaps used for process design or redesign projects.

1.2 From Lean and Six Sigma to Lean Six Sigma

Both Lean and Six Sigma have been separately and successfully deployed across the manufacturing and services sectors and have some shortcomings. The hybrid Lean Six Sigma (LSS) approach to continuous improvement has helped overcome the shortcomings (Sunder M 2013), and hence, its usage has exponentially increased in the past two decades. The claim that Lean and Six Sigma have a complementary relationship is widely accepted today in the corporate world. LSS has been acknowledged by more than 70% of Fortune 500 companies across various Services sectors (Chassin 2008). Though LSS is gaining momentum in industry, top-tier journals have published little research on this phenomenon. While many papers have appeared in the practitioner literature and specialized scholarly journals in this area, LSS needs an in-depth understanding to advance its theoretical development (Näslund 2013; Snee 2010). Scholarly inquiry into this management approach has been limited to view LSS merely as a CI practice. LSS has not attracted the same level of conversation about theory development and implications for competitive advantage as TQM (Powell 1995; Douglas and Judge 2001), and some researchers have recognized LSS as being distinct from TQM and various other well-known quality philosophies and practices (Furterer and Elshennawy 2005; Shafer and Moeller 2012). Secondly, while CI initiatives have been taken in both manufacturing and services organizations, the need for CI in services, especially in economies dominated by the services sector, is strongly justified. For instance, the services sector dominates the UK economy, contributing around 78% of GDP (as on 2015 per statistica.com). Since 2010, more than 80% of the USA's GDP has been contributed by services operations (Wang and Chen 2010). Even in emerging economies like India, the share of the services sector is expected to reach 62% by FY 2022.

1.3 Purpose and Scope of This Book

An overview of the publications pertaining to Lean Six Sigma for services shows that its applications in the BFS, ITS, telecom, education, and aviation/airline services sectors are in nascent stages. This book is scoped in the context of banking considering the importance of the BFS sector due to the reasons given below. Predominantly, BFS firms originate and facilitate financial transactions for circulation of funds. Their operations include creation, liquidation, transfer of ownership, and servicing or management of financial assets, raising funds by taking deposits or issuing securities, making loans, asset management, underwriting insurance, payments processing and settlements.

Further, LSS has been looked upon as an efficiency generation machine, and evidences from several field studies demonstrate its operational benefits. Practitioner research on this area shows that LSS synergizes the rapidness of Lean and robustness of Six Sigma to solve almost all operational problems in firms as a CI platform and practice. However, there is a significant gap in the literature of not looking at LSS from a strategic management perspective. Hence, this book is scoped to bridge this gap. Further, among several strategic management theories, the contemporary dynamic capabilities approach is apparently the latest which has attracted significant scholarly attention. Having its roots from the famous resource-based view and Schumpeterian works, research on the DCs approach has provided several implications for strategic management. Hence, this book is scoped to study LSS through a DCs lens to validate its fitness to be recognized as a DC.

Considering the pace and dominance of research on CI occurring across the USA and UK, this study has chosen cases pertaining to banks headquartered at the USA and UK (Wang and Chen 2010). However, globalization and the rise of multinational organizations have paved an opportunity to view organizations holistically with their global presence. Hence, it is evident that though the banks chosen for the study are headquartered at the USA and UK, their scattered global presence is taken into consideration (average presence across 32 countries across three multinational banks, with an average customer base of 55 million and net revenues worth 42.67 billion USD).

Purposive sampling, a non-probability sampling method suggested by Patton (1990), is used to select cases that span different contextual settings to increase generalizability. First, several global banks that have claimed to have recently started LSS deployment practice have been approached. Secondly, only those banks that have attempted either Lean or Six Sigma or both independently, before embarking upon their LSS journey are considered. Then, the selection is scoped to only those banks that serve customers across multiple banking streams (like retail banking, commercial banking, investment banking and wealth management). This filter was added to incorporate the diversity in processes of the banks. The purposive sampling helped to identify firms with varying diversity in their tenure, geographical and business spread, number of employees, stability of operations, and financial performance. More details about these are provided in the fore coming chapters. Figure 1.1 summarizes the scope of this book.

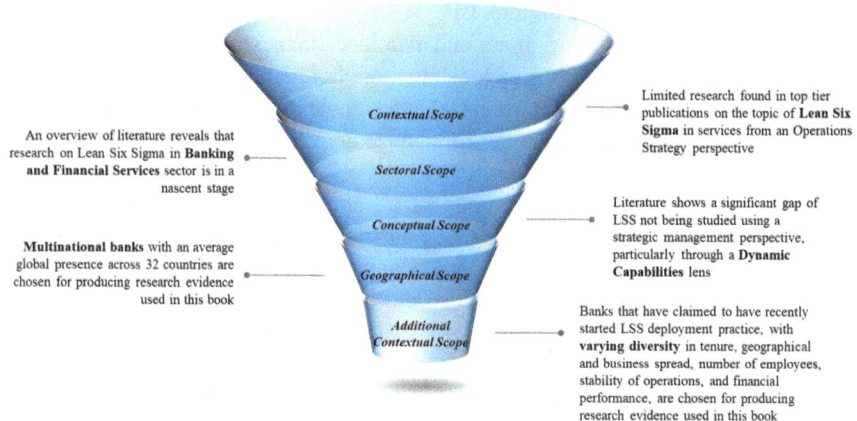

Fig. 1.1 Funnel diagram to illustrate the scope

1.4 What Can You Expect from This Book?

This book provides opportunities for researchers to conduct research on Lean Six Sigma related topics. It provides directions by pointing research gaps and potential applications of Lean Six Sigma in the services contexts. Secondly, this book presents case evidences of Lean Six Sigma project management in the banking context. The case organizations are carefully chosen to reflect the lessons learnt and subsequent discussions should trigger the realization of the value of LSS in managers for effective results. Thirdly, this book presents both operational and strategic orientations of Lean Six Sigma. While the case data that help us arrive findings and conclusions come from the banking sector, the findings allow generalizability beyond the BFS sector. However, this claim needs validation by future research. Finally, this book caters to the needs of both researchers (Ph.D scholars, research academicians, teachers in the fields of operations management and strategic management) and practitioners (CI practitioners, quality management leaders and corporate LSS aspirants) by contributing to both theory and applied thought leadership in the above-said discipline of management science.

The concept map presented in Fig. 1.2 shows how this book is organized to meet the above expectations. This book is organized into seven chapters. This chapter has provided the Introduction.

Chapter 2 sets a background by introducing key concepts across various related topics including service quality, competitive advantage in quality, CI, organizational learning, Lean, Six Sigma, and LSS. This chapter familiarizes the readers with these backgrounds so that, even if the reader does not have any pre-requisite knowledge about quality management, should be able to understand the rest of the contents of the book easily.

Chapter 3 presents an overview of banking services. This chapter provides readers with a fair understanding of banking sector, types of banking, practices in banking and how banks have been embarking quality management journeys in the past. This chapter also presents why CI is critical to banking, and how is it different from other sectors. Further, key performance indicators specific to BFS are discussed to provide directions to identify LSS opportunities in real-time.

Chapter 4 features a morphological analysis of literature on LSS for service. Morphological analysis being a systems thinking technique helps in classifying and integrating the literature of LSS for services into a framework, which is easy to understand. This chapter reveals 355 research gaps as a resource for scholars working in this area. It also provides an integrated system of knowledge encompassing several dimensions to present a holistic picture of LSS to the practitioners.

Chapter 5 presents three Lean Six Sigma case studies to explain the application of LSS project management in banking firms. By studying LSS project cases from three banks, this chapter presents lessons learned and implications. It concludes that the extent of applicability of LSS in banking depends on the interest, rigor and scope of banking operations. It establishes LSS project management as merely a subset of LSS deployment in banks. Both, tangible and intangible benefits of LSS are evident in the consumer banking context from the above real-world case evidences. This

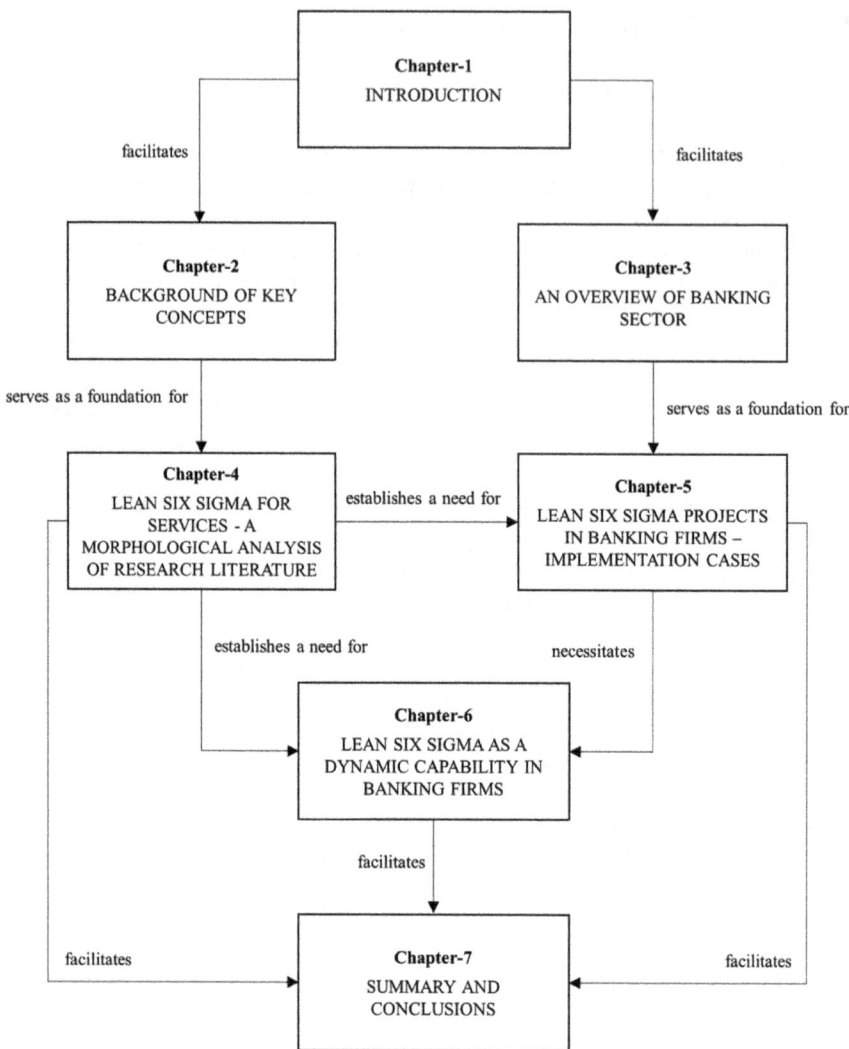

Fig. 1.2 Concept map showing the linkages of chapters of this book

chapter concludes with the affirmation that LSS needs to be understood using a systems perspective for moving away from a narrow project-only approach. An LSS project selection criterion is recommended. Further, important managerial implications discovered in this chapter include effective management of stakeholders and change leadership as essential elements of LSS project management in banks.

Chapter 6 challenges the traditional view of quality management and advocates a dynamic capabilities approach as a counter-intuitive approach to management. This chapter establishes LSS as a DC using longitudinal case evidence. Using an iterative triangulation method to reflect its strategic value toward creating competitive advantage in quality, Chapter 6 evaluates LSS to be recognized as a DC. Using a purposive sample of three global banks, the primary data was collected using multiple rounds of interviews with select top- and mid-management personnel, site visits, participation in LSS project meetings and execution, study of management archives and reported data on public domains. For triangulation, this primary data was synthesized with the results noted from the research literature on both LSS and DCs, which were studied independently by previous researchers. A cross-comparison of the case studies was performed to derive useful findings. The novel CI approach reinforces the strategic orientations of LSS beyond its operational applications as a CI practice.

Finally, Chapter 7 summarizes this book with appropriate conclusions, limitations and contributions to the body of knowledge.

References

Albliwi, S., Antony, J., Abdul Halim Lim, S., & van der Wiele, T. (2014). Critical failure factors of Lean Six Sigma: A systematic literature review. *International Journal of Quality & Reliability Management, 31*(9), 1012–1030.

Anand, G., Ward, P. T., Tatikonda, M. V., & Schilling, D. A. (2009). Dynamic capabilities through continuous improvement infrastructure. *Journal of Operations Management, 27*(6), 444–461.

Barney, J. (1991). Special theory forum the resource-based model of the firm: Origins, implications, and prospects. *Journal of Management, 17*(1), 97–98.

Barreto, I. (2010). Dynamic capabilities: A review of past research and an agenda for the future. *Journal of management, 36*(1), 256–280.

Benner, M. J., & Tushman, M. L. (2003). Exploitation, exploration, and process management: The productivity dilemma revisited. *Academy of Management Review, 28*(2), 238–256.

Chassin, R. (2008). The Six Sigma initiative at Mount Sinai medical center. *Mount Sinai Journal of Medicine: A Journal of Translational and Personalized Medicine: A Journal of Translational and Personalized Medicine, 75*(1), 45–52.

DeFEO, J. A. (2000). Six Sigma: Perfection is possible in meeting customer needs. *Handbook of Business Strategy, 1*(1), 153–162.

Douglas, T. J., & Judge, W. Q., Jr. (2001). Total quality management implementation and competitive advantage: The role of structural control and exploration. *Academy of Management Journal, 44*(1), 158–169.

Fitzgerald, K.R. (1997). *Chrysler training helps suppliers trim the fat*. Available at http://findarticles.com/p/articles/mi_hb3381/is_199709/ai_n8127241/?tag¼col1;co-competitors (accessed September 2, 2014).

Flynn, B. B., & Saladin, B. (2001). Further evidence on the validity of the theoretical models underlying the Baldrige criteria. *Journal of Operations Management, 19*(6), 617–652.

Flynn, B. B., Schroeder, R. G., & Sakakibara, S. (1994). A framework for quality management research and an associated measurement instrument. *Journal of Operations Management, 11*(4), 339–366.

Furterer, S., & Elshennawy, A. K. (2005). Implementation of TQM and Lean Six Sigma tools in local government: A framework and a case study. *Total Quality Management & Business Excellence, 16*(10), 1179–1191.

Hannan, M. T., & Freeman, J. (1984). Structural inertia and organizational change. *American Sociological Review*, 149–164.

Lucas, J. M. (2002). The essential six sigma. *Quality Progress, 35*(1), 27–31.

Makadok, R. (2001). Toward a synthesis of the resource-based and dynamic-capability views of rent creation. *Strategic Management Journal, 22*(5), 387–401.

Martínez-Costa, M., Choi, T. Y., Martínez, J. A., & Martínez-Lorente, A. R. (2009). ISO 9000/1994, ISO 9001/2000 and TQM: The performance debate revisited. *Journal of Operations Management, 27*(6), 495–511.

Näslund, D. (2013). Lean and Six Sigma–critical success factors revisited. *International Journal of Quality and Service Sciences, 5*(1), 86–100.

Patton, M.Q. (1990). *Qualitative evaluation and research methods* (2nd ed.). Newbury Park, CA: Sage.

Porter, M. E. (1985). Technology and competitive advantage. *The Journal of Business Strategy, 5*(3), 60.

Powell, T. C. (1995). Total quality management as competitive advantage: A review and empirical study. *Strategic Management Journal, 16*(1), 15–37.

Prahalad, C. K., & Hamel, G. (1990). Core competency concept. *Harvard Business Review, 64*(3), 70–92.

Pyzdek, T. (2003). *The Six Sigma*. Estados Unidos: Mcgraw-Hill.

Rawabdeh, I. A. (2005). A model for the assessment of waste in job shop environments. *International Journal of Operations & Production Management, 25*(8), 800–822.

Schilke, O., Hu, S., & Helfat, C. E. (2018). Quo vadis, dynamic capabilities? A content-analytic review of the current state of knowledge and recommendations for future research. *Academy of Management Annals, 12*(1), 390–439.

Shafer, S. M., & Moeller, S. B. (2012). The effects of Six Sigma on corporate performance: An empirical investigation. *Journal of Operations Management, 30*(7–8), 521–532.

Sharma, A. (2014). What is lean manufacturing. *International Journal of Sciences, 3*(9), 44–49.

Snee, R. D. (2010). Lean Six Sigma–getting better all the time. *International Journal of Lean Six Sigma, 1*(1), 9–29.

Stewart, J. R., & Meyers, F. E. (2002). *Motion time study for lean manufacturing*. Englewood Cliffs, NJ: Prentice-Hall.

Su, H. C., Linderman, K., Schroeder, R. G., & Van de Ven, A. H. (2014). A comparative case study of sustaining quality as a competitive advantage. *Journal of Operations Management, 32*(7–8), 429–445.

Sunder M, V. (2013). Synergies of Lean Six Sigma. *IUP Journal of Operations Management, 12*(1), 21.

Sunder M, V., & Prashar, A. (2020). Empirical examination of critical failure factors of continuous improvement deployments: stage-wise results and a contingency theory perspective. *International Journal of Production Research*, 1–22. https://doi.org/10.1080/00207543.2020.1727044.

Teece, D. J. (2007). Explicating dynamic capabilities: the nature and microfoundations of (sustainable) enterprise performance. *Strategic Management Journal, 28*(13), 1319–1350.

Teece, D. J., Pisano, G., & Shuen, A. (1997). Dynamic capabilities and strategic management. *Strategic Management Journal, 18*(7), 509–533.

Wang, F. K., & Chen, K. S. (2010). Applying Lean Six Sigma and TRIZ methodology in banking services. *Total Quality Management, 21*(3), 301–315.

Ward, P. T., & Duray, R. (2000). Manufacturing strategy in context: environment, competitive strategy and manufacturing strategy. *Journal of operations management, 18*(2), 123–138.

Womack, J. P., & Jones, D. T. (1997). Lean thinking—banish waste and create wealth in your corporation. *Journal of the Operational Research Society, 48*(11), 1148.

Zollo, M., & Winter, S. G. (2002). Deliberate learning and the evolution of dynamic capabilities. *Organization Science, 13*(3), 339–351.

Background of Key Concepts 2

Quality management has been the backbone of success for several organizations. A good product or a service always attracts customers, and hence, quality management is no more a good-to-have factor but a must-be requirement to attain competitive advantage. During the past few decades, "quality" has become a major area of interest for practitioners and researchers owing to its strong impact on performance in organizations, lower costs, customer satisfaction, customer loyalty and profitability (Sunder M 2016a). Quality has indeed evaded a standard definition because quality tends to depend on the context, especially in the service environment and can often be based subjectively on several parameters like the industry, segment, customer needs, organization culture, time, etc. However, the works of Deming, Crosby, and Juran did provide a foundation for defining relevant criteria to establish quality as a management science. According to Crosby, quality excellence means "conformance to requirements" and quality must be defined as a measurable action based on tangible targets rather than based on experience or opinions (Crosby 1979). Juran mentioned that quality excellence is a concept of managerial breakthrough and could be achieved through the quality trilogy (Juran 1986). Deming suggested that quality excellence could not be achieved in organizations without educating leadership on importance of quality–obligations, principles, and methods (Krishnaiah and Rao 1988). The research on quality excellence has been building over the theories of these three masters. From past two decades, researchers have seen a paradigm shift of viewing quality excellence from manufacturing to services. There has been incessant effort made by researchers to understand the quality perspectives across service industry and banking sector is not an exception.

Different concepts, viz., service quality, continuous improvement (CI), organizational learning, lean services, six sigma for services, and a brief overview of Lean Six Sigma (LSS) are discussed in this Chapter as they are relevant to this book and help develop and provide a conceptual foundation for the work presented in fore coming Chapters. As can be easily observed, the theories belong to different research areas are yet to be integrated but help offer a unique perspective to this book. The task of integrating the theories is done conceptually as well as empirically across the Chapters, and this will be pointed out in the respective Chapters as and when necessary. The integration significantly contributes to the body of knowledge concerning CI for creating competitive advantage in services.

2.1 A Brief Overview of Service Quality

The evolution and maturity of research in the area of service operations have led to many new perspectives of the core production-oriented operations management (OM) field which was associated solely with the manufacturing sector till the 1980s (Johnston 1999). Today, the services sector plays an important role in the global economy. The services sector dominates the UK economy, contributing around 78% of GDP (as on 2015 per statistica.com). Since 2010, more than 80% of the USA's GDP has been contributed by services operations (Wang and Chen 2010). Even in emerging economies like India, the share of the services sector is expected to reach 68% by 2022.

The inherent characteristics of services like heterogeneity, intangibility, perishability, and inseparability contribute to greater inconsistency in managing customer experiences. Firstly, heterogeneity reflects the potential for high variability in service delivery and can introduce a benefit and point of differentiation. Second, the degree of intangibility is the means of distinguishing between products and services, and the degree of tangibility has implications for the ease with which consumers can evaluate services. Thirdly, services cannot be stored and carried forward to a future time period, and this feature is called as perishability. Perishability can be defined as a "time-dependent" and "time-important" characteristic unique to services. Finally, inseparability reflects the simultaneous delivery and consumption of services, and it enables to shape the performance and quality of the respective services.

"Service quality" is an important area of increasing interest in service operations. The seminal text of Lewis and Booms (1983) defined service quality as "a measure of how well the service level delivered matches customer expectations, i.e., confirming to customer expectations on a consistent basis." Increasing customer demands, competitive pressures and rising operational costs have created a compelling reason for this cause. Literature shows evidence of several service quality models. A few of them include the technical and functional quality model, GAP model, model for customers' perceptions of service quality or SERVQUAL, extended SERVQUAL model, attribute service quality model, synthesized model of service quality, service performance model or SERVPERF, ideal value model of service quality, evaluated performance and normed quality model, model of perceived service quality and satisfaction, service quality-customer value-customer satisfaction model, mediator model, internal service quality model, internal service quality DEA model, and model of e-service quality.

Management thinkers have noted that increase in service quality increases revenue by making services more striking. A few operations management scholars noted that this quality advantage was not only an enabler for reducing cost by increasing efficiency but also a front-runner in creating a market advantage (Flynn et al. 1994). Quality enables other competitive dimensions, and quality performance leads to creation and sustenance of competitive advantage in firms. Quality performance is not merely delivering the required output to the customers but a management strategy to enhance and continuously align the organizational resources, processes, and systems in a way that quality becomes a continuous and inherent part of the ways of working (Sunder M and Antony 2018).

While achieving high quality performance at one point in time indicates a high level of performance, it does not indicate high consistency of performance. A high consistency of performance is achieving "collective outcomes of a certain minimum level repeatedly." High consistency of quality performance therefore indicates lower variance in quality performance. Organizations that sustain a competitive advantage in quality should not only achieve a high level of quality performance at a point in time but also do it consistently over time.

2.2 Continuous Improvement

CI has become the backbone to gain the quality advantage in firms, and several CI philosophies and practices for quality management have been devised and studied. A few of them include total quality management (TQM), Lean, ISO 9000, Malcolm Baldrige award and Six Sigma. Service organizations have been adapting these CI practices for multiple operational benefits, viz., to improve their service levels and to impart the culture of CI for effective customer service and cost reduction. Significant contributions have been made by researchers on these subjects across various service sectors including healthcare, banking and financial services, hospitality services, airlines, and information technology services (Sunder M et al. 2018; George 2003).

The ability to consistently improve current processes and learn new ones is termed as "continuous improvement" (Ittner and Larcker 1997). CI as a concept has emerged from many fields including the quality movement of 1980s, socio-technical systems, efficiency creation, operational performance, design thinking, goal-centric theories, process theory, human relations movement, etc. CI programs have evolved over the years and have been associated with the adoption of Lean manufacturing techniques, TQM, Six Sigma, business excellence, customer services excellence, and other quality management practices. An ideal CI program should serve three purposes for the holistic benefit of an organization, viz., (1) provide tangible benefits including improved operational performance leading to cost efficiencies, (2) enable a culture of CI in organizations, and (3) lead to the development of competitive advantage in firms. In the era of globalization, researchers have increasingly recognized the importance of CI practices for providing value to customers and cost arbitrage to the management.

Among other CI practices, Lean and Six Sigma have received greater attention from both researchers and practitioners across the world. The multiple-level collective problem-solving approach of Lean, tapping the resourcefulness across all levels, and stimulating the appropriate management behaviors toward self-discovery, exploring new knowledge and continuous learning, rationalizes its candidature to be an important organizational capability. The heterogenous features of Six Sigma like structured problem-solving for CI, promotion of quality culture, emergence in knowledge creation, diffusion, and retention, being a strategy for employee engagement for organizational learning, substantiates it as a key capability in organizations. Further, both Lean and Six Sigma help to transform and integrate operations within the firm and across the supply chain, thus enhancing the firm's ability to make cohesive and quick process changes that could align with the environmental indications. Their synergetic integration as Lean Six Sigma (LSS) has been relatively new, widely used in service sectors and gained a lot of attraction among both scholarly and practitioner groups.

2.3 Organizational Learning in the Context of CI

"Organization learning" is defined as a change in the organizations' knowledge that increases the range of its potential behaviors (Argote 2013). It could be argued that learning need not essentially reflect in behaviors but it would enable cultural changes. For example, when general electric implemented Six Sigma and made it mandatory for every employee to be aware of it and contribute to the cause, there were reported cultural changes in organizational structure, decision making, hiring practices, and talent management. Realizing the importance of organizational learning, firms use exploration or exploitation strategies. Explorative approaches like vicarious learning (learning from other market players rather than direct experience), experimentation (learning through controlled experiments), grafting (combining different pieces of knowledge together to enable cross structure learning), etc., are well recognized in the literature. Contrastingly, exploitation strategies of organizational learning focus on enhancing or refining existing knowledge to address known problems concerning ideation, efficiency, tactical automation, etc.

CI practices focus on both organizational (processes) and individual (behavioral) improvements via exploration and exploitation. Su et al. (2014) term this type of learning as meta-learning and state that it refers to the "reflection on and inquiry into the process of learning at the individual and group levels." CI in an organization not only improves its processes but also enables organizational learning through structured thinking leading to problem solving. This further leads to disciplined behaviors which enable firms to create processes and systems that produce high quality outputs aligned with customer expectations. If implemented in its right form, a CI strategy leads to organizational learning to instill quality and a customer centric culture triggering emotional productivity in the workforce. This is aligned with Fredrick Taylor's thinking of emotional and non-emotional behaviors at work, where he claims that high emotional productivity implies that people behave efficiently in support of production with an appetite for continuous learning. In other words, they enjoy what they do and continuously share and learn the derived knowledge, and hence, produce effective output toward economic growth and prosperity.

2.4 Lean Services—Successes and Shortcomings

The origins of Lean thinking can be traced to the shop-floors of Toyota Motor Corporation. Through their book *The Machine that Changed the World*, Womack et al. (1990) popularized the Lean concept in the manufacturing sector. Lean practices diffused into American firms in the 1970s and then across the globe swiftly. Lean production is an integrated system that is intended to maximize capacity utilization and minimize buffer inventories of a given operation through minimizing system variability. The early works on Lean conceptualized the Lean philosophy, which was earlier known as "Toyota Production System." However, these contributions were short on details and lacked practical relevance. Later, in their book *Lean Thinking*, Womack and Jones (1996) structured Lean concepts into five categories: value, value stream, flow, pull, and perfection, which later came to be known as Lean principles. Lean focusses on maximizing process velocity, analyzes process flow and delay times, centers on identification of non-value-added activities (waste) and their elimination, and reduces the cost of complexity.

Over several years, scholarly research has published several articles that focused on both, the philosophical and practical sides of Lean, highlighting its success. Alongside manufacturing, Lean has gained significant attention in the services sectors as well. Lean tools such as value-stream mapping, 5S, and waste analysis have been relatively easily transferred from the manufacturing to retail supply contexts due to the common focus on product flows. Though Lean originated from the manufacturing sector, its significant potential for services has also been realized in past two decades. As a successful CI strategy, Lean has demonstrably helped service organizations achieve on-time delivery of the right quality and quantity of services to satisfy customers.

Alongside its successes, Lean has shortcomings on several counts and has encountered adverse criticism from researchers. According to Spear (2004), many organizations wrongly perceived Lean as a set of tools and practices rather than as a CI philosophy. This misconception led to confusion in many organizations in their attempts to motivate employees to participate in Lean programs. Critics argued that Lean is not the only effective solution for customer satisfaction, and Lean by itself is not all perfect. Toyota's performance in Europe in the recent past has often been lacking. According to Bhasin (2015), "[…] even Toyota in Japan, failed to produce in several circumstances, cars to actual customer order." Others found that the approach to implement Lean produces a cascading effect of problems, beginning with lack of senior management commitment and going down to lack of total employee participation. It could be argued that senior management commitment is essential for any and all CI initiatives and not just for Lean. However, the bottom-up approach of Lean makes it more challenging to gain organizational leaders' commitment toward it. It was also noticed that in a few Lean implementations, top management avoids accountability when problems arise, letting it filter downwards onto the lower levels of the hierarchy. This view of Lean contradicts the fundamental CI principle of spreading a quality mind-set within organizations. However, a few authors who have contributed to Lean literature have highlighted the top-down approach of Hoshin Kanri (policy deployment), which is a method for ensuring that the strategic goals of a company drive top-down progress and action by focusing on eliminating the waste that comes from inconsistent direction and poor communication (Kondo 1998). A few other Lean thinkers supplemented this literature with "Catchball," which refers to the bidirectional top-down, bottom-up process through which objectives, plans, and metrics are spread among levels and departments. Another drawback of Lean is that it is not a data-driven approach unlike other CI programs including Six Sigma. The use of a wide variety of management practices in Lean implementation validates the requirement for various generic performance indicators, and there is a need to measure them effectively. There are a few arguments that some of the Lean principles like pull do not add any value within the services industry. This is because pull is inherent in the nature of services, and Lean has nothing new to add here.

We can observe that Lean has been very successfully deployed in the services sector although its limitations have been stated in the literature and noted in practice. The organizational learning resulting from Lean and its role in building a CI culture reflect Lean's strategic implications as an organizational capability. Like Lean, another CI method, Six Sigma, was promoted first in the manufacturing sector and then in the services sector. Six Sigma has been extensively applied in and by various types of firms, and the results have been reported widely by practitioners.

2.5 Six Sigma in Services—Successes and Shortcomings

The Six Sigma movement, which originated from Motorola, has spread to other organizations determined to realize CI. Many Fortune 500 firms adopted Six Sigma as a practice (Nakhai and Neves 2009). Six Sigma integrates business-level performance, process measures, and project metrics into a systematic process so that leaders can manage organizational operations quantitatively and transform the business strategy into operational tasks. Till the 1990s, Six Sigma was understood solely as a statistical term used for restricting process defects to 3.4 per million opportunities. During the last two decades, it has evolved from being a statistical problem-solving technique to become a management strategy and ultimately a refined CI philosophy. Six Sigma not only focuses on reducing process variations

2.5 Six Sigma in Services—Successes and Shortcomings

and defects but also encourages creating a process thinking mind-set in organizations. Six Sigma improvement projects follow a structured problem-solving approach that takes its roots from the Plan-Do-Check-Act cycle. It suggests two project management approaches, namely Define-Measure-Analyze-Improve-Control (DMAIC) and Define-Measure-Analyze-Design-Verify (DMADV), for eliminating the root causes of problems. Scholars defined Six Sigma in three ways:

(a) a business process to improve a firm's bottom-line and customer satisfaction
(b) a statistical discipline to improve quality in organizations by significantly reducing defects and variation, and
(c) a CI strategy that focuses on reducing process variations and defects, toward creating a process thinking mind-set in organizations.

Recent developments have included increased organizational and academic interest in the Six Sigma approach. According to Michael Hammer, the co-founder of Six Sigma, at least 25% of Fortune 200 companies claimed that they implemented Six Sigma programs seriously. Leading firms like GE, Ford, Honeywell, and American Express claimed that it transformed their organizations. Six Sigma has been embraced by many big services firms such as JP Morgan, American Express, Lloyds TSB, Egg, Citibank, Zurich Financial Services (Antony 2006). Though it originated from manufacturing, there is evidence in the literature that Six Sigma has been adopted and applied outside the anufacturing sector too. There are several recent success stories of Six Sigma in the services sector published in various journals as an evidence.

Like Lean, Six Sigma has also encountered adverse criticism due to its limitations. Though the practitioner literature provides considerable evidence of substantial cost reduction and other benefits from Six Sigma, questions on whether these benefits sufficiently exceeded the costs of adoption have been raised (Swink and Jacobs 2012). Stories from companies like 3 M and Home Depot indicate that organizational leaders believe that Six Sigma practices may constrict innovation to drive growth. Many Six Sigma programs failed due to wrong selection of projects. Not all projects qualify to be run with Six Sigma methodology. According to Adams (2003), "doing Six Sigma training before project identification is the classic – getting the cart before the horse." Further to this, a few critics perceived that the define and control phases were areas of weakness in the DMAIC methodology and that unconventional execution of these phases is suggested.

The prioritization of projects in many services companies is still based on pure subjective judgement, and it is argued that there was no standardized procedure for accrediting Six Sigma programs. This entertains organizations to claim that they are following Six Sigma although it may not be true in many cases. An important limitation of Six Sigma is the amount of investment made by firms on niche skilled Six Sigma belts for deployment. Yet another challenge of implementing Six Sigma is the usage of statistical techniques during projects, which management feels difficult to comprehend. Another shortcoming is that the relationship between Six Sigma and organizational culture/learning has not been explored yet in research.

Moreover, many organizations still perceive Six Sigma as a pure statistical toolkit rather than as a management strategy, and there is no significant work found in academic literature to overcome this misconception. There is very little room for clarifying the confusion in the literature as to what constitutes Six Sigma theory and how it integrates with other CI strategies.

2.6 A Brief Overview of Lean Six Sigma

LSS is a result of the integration of Lean and Six Sigma and consequent synergies. As a hybrid methodology, LSS has bridged the critical gaps and shortcomings of Lean and Six Sigma noted by several critics. For example, Lean cannot bring a process under statistical control, and Six Sigma cannot reduce process speed or reduce invested capital (George 2003). LSS integrates the rapidness of Lean and robustness of Six Sigma to result in emergent properties and is now an enthusiastically accepted CI approach across industries. It balances the top-down approach of Six Sigma with the bottom-up approach of Lean making quality everyone's job in the organization. LSS stands out compared to its predecessors due to three unique features, viz., (1) integration of the human and process elements of improvement, (2) clear focus on getting bottom-line results quickly, and (3) a structured problem-solving method that sequences and links improvement tools and techniques with strategy into an overall approach. Predominantly, quality leaders including Six Sigma Master Black Belts need to re-invent their role in an organization and move from "quality control" and "quality improvement" to "interpreters of business strategy" and drive the integration of all quality processes, metrics, tools, and accountancy systems to optimize the performance of all departments, providing quality training and lending leadership support to the overall LSS program. A Black Belt plays the role of a dedicated project manager alongside trainings and change management, and Green belts are operational staff who get trained in LSS methods to conduct projects alongside their routine jobs.

The initial usage of the term "Lean Six Sigma" could be ascribed to the book *Lean Six Sigma: Combining Six Sigma Quality with Lean Speed* by George (2002). Although it is possible that the term "LSS" could have been used even before, no evidence was found in the scholarly literature until 2002. From then on, LSS has been widely embraced by various firms as a CI strategy. According to a recent study, LSS has been acknowledged by more than 70% of Fortune 500 companies. Despite industry acceptance of LSS, there is only limited academic research on this topic. A Google Scholar search of the exact phrase "Lean Six Sigma" finds ~26,600 results with the phrase occurring anywhere in the article and 2820 results with the phrase occurring in the title of the article. 52% of these 2820 results (i.e., 1470 publications) were published in the last five years (i.e., between 2012 and 2017). This shows a considerable recent increase in academic interest on this emerging topic.

An overview of LSS literature reveals its successful application, operational perspectives, and managerial implications in firms. The reported benefits of LSS application revealed outcomes like efficiency improvement, cost reduction, revenue generation, quality and productivity improvement, risk reduction, customer and employee satisfaction, increase in innovation quotient in the firm, error reduction, etc.

While deploying LSS in organizations, it is important to follow a structured deployment framework for success. The first step in this journey includes establishing a need for LSS. This is an important first step as this lays the foundation of the further next steps in deployment. According to Wickens (1999), it is a common mistake to attempt any reengineering practice without the requisite leadership and could have tremendous negative effects. When change has to take place, there are multiple error possibilities that leadership team can make, and missing to establish a need to change is the primary one, following missing to communicate about the urgency. From an organizational deployment perspective, it is essential that top management is committed to LSS.

Active participation of senior management is essential in the success of any improvement methods within any organization irrespective of industry, nature, or size. Hence, the primary step to deploy LSS in firms is to establish a need for LSS through leadership. In fact, many people strongly suggest LSS must be launched at the executive level because it proves to be more successful when it is led by top executives in an organization. Reputed firms like GE, Honeywell, Bank of America, Motorola, Bombardier, etc., are several examples of companies in which successful implementation of LSS are closely connected to a thorough commitment by top management. The active role of leadership has been widely reported as a critical success factor for implementation and deployment of LSS (Sunder M and Antony 2018).

LSS is not all about managing projects or applying a toolkit for improvement. LSS is a culture building vehicle for imbibing quality excellence. It needs to be looked as a mindset and a strategic initiative rather than a tactical gadget. Upon setting the need for LSS, the second important step is to align it with the organization's vision, infrastructure, and goals/milestones. This step establishes the readiness for LSS. Thirdly, LSS enables systemic training of employees and correct selection of CI projects for further execution using DMAIC or DMADV methods. These training and accreditation efforts, though not standardized across the firms, still feature the Six Sigma belting system (Green, Black, and Master Black Belts) with groups of niche skilled consultants, unlike a few firms in which attempts to develop in-house expertise on LSS have been dominant. Table 2.1 shows the description of various activities that are carried out within each phase of the DMAIC problem-solving methodology (Sunder M 2016b).

A few other articles highlighted implementation issues, viz., readiness factors, challenges and critical success/failure factors, concerning LSS. Other authors focused on LSS project management, frameworks, tools and techniques, and their evaluation methods. An in-depth systematic review of LSS in services, represented within a morphological analysis framework, is presented in Chap. 4.

Table 2.1 DMAIC common tools

Define	Measure	Analyse	Improve	Control
1. Develop Project charter 2. Identify relevant stakeholders 3. Perform VOC and identify the project metric 4. Select team and launch the project	5. Define the current process mapping 6. Perform the Gauge study to validate the measurement system 7. Perform Waste analysis 8. Measure the process capability	9. Brainstorm and identify the causes 10. Develop cause and effect relationships 11. Determine and validate causes using various graphical and statistical tools	12. Identify improvements 13. Create an improvement plan 14. Establish performance targets 15. gain stakeholder approval and implement changes	16. Measure results and manage change 17. Report and communicate improvements to gain buy-in for future 18. Identify replication opportunities and develop future plans

The above discussions have provided overviews of various relevant concepts with the purpose of providing a theoretical background to this book.

References

Adams, C. W. (2003). *Six Sigma Deployment*. New York, NY: Elsevier Science.
Antony, J. (2006). Six sigma for service processes. *Business Process Management Journal, 12*(2), 234–248.
Argote, L. (2013). Organization learning: A theoretical framework. In Organizational learning (pp. 31–56). Springer, Boston, MA.
Bhasin, S. (2015). *Lean management beyond manufacturing*. New York, NY: Springer.
Crosby, P. B. (1979). *Quality is free: The art of making quality certain* (Vol. 94). New York: McGraw-Hill.
Flynn, B. B., Schroeder, R. G., & Sakakibara, S. (1994). A framework for quality management research and an associated measurement instrument. *Journal of Operations Management, 11*(4), 339–366.
George, M. L. (2002). Lean six sigma: Combining six sigma quality with lean speed. In M. L. George. McGraw-Hill, USA.
George, M. L. (2003). How to use Lean speed and Six Sigma quality to improve services and transactions.
Ittner, C. D., & Larcker, D. F. (1997). The performance effects of process management techniques. *Management Science, 43*(4), 522–534.
Johnston, R. (1999). Service transaction analysis: Assessing and improving the customer's experience. *Managing Service Quality: An International Journal, 9*(2), 102–109.
Juran, J. M. (1986). The quality trilogy. *Quality Progress, 19*(8), 19–24.
Kondo, Y. (1998). Hoshin kanri-a participative way of quality management in Japan. *The TQM Magazine, 10*(6), 425–431.
Krishnaiah, P. R., & Rao, C. R. (Eds.). (1988). *Quality control and reliability*. New York, NY: North-Holland.
Lewis, R. C., & Booms, B. H. (1983). *The marketing of service quality in emerging perspectives on service marketing* (pp. 99–107). Chicago: AMA.
Nakhai, B., & Neves, J. S. (2009). The challenges of six sigma in improving service quality. *International Journal of Quality & Reliability Management, 26*(7), 663–684.

References

Spear, S. J. (2004). Learning to lead at Toyota. *Harvard Business Review, 82*(5), 78–91.

Su, H. C., Linderman, K., Schroeder, R. G., & Van de Ven, A. H. (2014). A comparative case study of sustaining quality as a competitive advantage. *Journal of Operations Management, 32*(7–8), 429–445.

Sunder M, V. (2016a). Constructs of quality in higher education services. *International Journal of Productivity and Performance Management, 65*(8), 1091–1111.

Sunder M, V. (2016b). Rejects reduction in a retail bank using Lean Six Sigma. *Production Planning & Control, 27*(14), 1131–1142.

Sunder M, V., & Antony, J. (2018). A conceptual Lean Six Sigma framework for quality excellence in higher education institutions. International Journal of Quality & Reliability Management.

Swink, M., & Jacobs, B. W. (2012). Six Sigma adoption: Operating performance impacts and contextual drivers of success. *Journal of Operations Management, 30*(6), 437–453.

Wang, F. K., & Chen, K. S. (2010). Applying Lean Six Sigma and TRIZ methodology in banking services. *Total Quality Management, 21*(3), 301–315.

Wickens, P. (1999). Energise your enterprise. Purdue University Press.

Womack, J., & Jones, D. (1996). *Lean thinking: Banish waste and create wealth in your corporation*. New York, NY: Simon & Schuster.

Womack, J., Jones, D., & Roos, D. P. et al. (1990). *The machine that changed the world*. New York: RA.

An Overview of Banking Sector 3

A bank holds assets for its clients, with a promise the money may be withdrawn if the individual or business needs them back. In general, the banking and financial services sector is the section of the economy devoted to (a) holding of financial assets for others, (b) investing those financial assets as leverage to create more wealth, and (c) regulation of those activities by government agencies.

BFS firms originate and facilitate financial transactions for the circulation of funds. Their operations include creation, liquidation, transfer of ownership, and servicing or management of financial assets, raising funds by taking deposits or issuing securities, making loans, asset management, underwriting insurance, payments processing, and settlements. BFS operations include provision of savings and transactional accounts, mortgages, personal loans, debit cards, and credit cards, etc. Most consumers utilize local branch banking services, which provide onsite customer service for all of the retail customer's banking needs. Through local branch locations, financial representatives provide customer service and financial advice. These financial representatives are also the lead contacts for underwriting applications related to credit-approved products. In the current digital era, a movement toward Internet finance banking operations has also broadly expanded the offerings for retail banking customers. Several online banks now provide banking services to customers purely through Internet and mobile applications. These banks offer nearly all of the accounts and services provided by traditional banks, often with lower fees from reduced banking branch expenses. A few distinctive characteristics of BFS operations are:

- Fungible products involving an extensive use of technology
- High volumes and heterogeneity of clients
- Repeated service encounters
- Long-term contractual relationships between customers and firms
- Customers' sense of well-being closely intertwined with services quality
- Use of intermediaries
- Convergence of operations, finance, and marketing.

3.1 An Overview of Global Banking Picture

In general, banks are classified into four categories—commercial banks, small finance banks, payments banks, and cooperative banks. Further, commercial banks can be classified into public sector banks, private sector banks, foreign banks, and regional rural banks; cooperative banks are classified into urban cooperative and rural cooperative banks. In a few developed countries like the USA, this classification also means retail banks, wholesale banks, and investment banks. Retail banking refers to that banking which targets individuals, and the main focus of such banks is retail customer, whereas wholesale banking refers to that banking which targets corporate customers and their main focus is providing services to corporate clients. On the other hand, investment banking is a special segment of banking operation that helps individuals or organizations raise capital and provide financial consultancy services (like mergers and acquisitions) to them. They act as intermediaries between security issuers and investors and help new firms to go public (e.g., asset management, equities management, etc.).

The middle and 1990s witnessed great innovations in financial reforms, restructuring, convergence, and globalization, etc. As a consequence of globalization, the banking sector has witnessed significant changes in their operational ways of working. Moving away from primarily cross-border flows to a system with more internationally diversified ownership of banks, banking sector has evolved in the past two decades. The impetus for the evolution of banking varies by player, time, and country. An overview of global picture reveals that, according to The Banker's Top 1000 World Banks Ranking for 2018, total assets reached $124 trillion (Lessambo 2020). Total assets in the USA reached a peak of $17.5 trillion in 2018. In the Asia-Pacific region, the growth of Chinese banks has been the most stunning development in the last decade. The world's four largest banks in 2018 are Chinese. However, many European banks have become smaller, retrenching from international markets, and exiting former profitable businesses. The top five European banks dropped from $60 billion in 2007 to $17.5 billion in 2017 (Arnold 2018). With these changes dominating the banking sector, BFS firms have moved to the ways of transformation. From being merely on a customer service mind-set, they have started moving into a change mind-set that enables newer and better ways of serving customers. Thus, banks have realized the need for CI toward this effect.

A recent market study report published by McKinsey reports three important drivers for CI in banks. First, there is a notable decline in customer loyalty and an increasing tendency for consumers to hop across remote and physical channels and split their decision journey. This rapidly shifting consumer behavior calls for potentially a complete revamp of processes. Second, rapid advances in technology and related infrastructure (e.g., mobile communications and big data) will cause greater competitive pressures, with newer players leapfrogging competition and levelling the playing field. Finally, an uncertain and volatile macroeconomic environment is affecting revenue growth and increasing potential risks. The direct customer contact opportunity associated with the consumer banks also offers a risk of consistently keeping the customers happy. This not only becomes a need for delight but also a need for survival at times. Further, the risk of fraud associated with digital banking products creates a compelling need for quality excellence in consumer banks. Hence, CI of processes using structured OM methods like LSS becomes essential in this context. Though the applicability of LSS is evident in the services sector through various published case studies and action research papers in scholarly journals, research on the use of LSS in the consumer banking sector deserves greater attention.

3.2 An Overview of LSS in Banking

Practitioners' research shows that BFS organizations have changed their ways of working by adopting LSS over the last decade. LSS deployment holds unique and great promise (mentioned below) for realizing CI in the BFS sector.

- BFS organizations generally work on heavy customer databases. Many retail banks deal with tons and tons of customer data which gets launched on their computer servers making it accessible to many bank staff. With heavy databases, the complexity of maintenance becomes challenging. While the big data analytics and associated technologies facilitate this maintenance, it becomes essential to align these with the fundamental prerequisites like data cleaning, structuring, and storage. All these data and associated activities should help banks to learn patterns for better customer service. It should lead to directions in customer service excellence which should evolve with the evolving customer needs. Consequently, they should use structured analysis for understanding and prioritizing evolving customer needs and preventing failure. LSS tools, such as the Kano model, quality function deployment, and benchmarking, fulfill this purpose. Kano model, for example, is an LSS tool that helps to prioritize the customer expectations translated to critical-to-quality (CTQ) metrics or KPIs. It enables the directional classification of customer needs based on the characteristics of the services and products offered. Kano model analysis categorizes customer needs to three categories, namely the must-be needs, one-dimensional needs, and attractive needs. While the must-be needs are the first priority metrics to be improved and monitored, one-dimensional and attractive needs become second and third priority categories of CTQs. This way it helps to identify which projects of CI should be taken up for further stages of improvement.
- Process performance measurement includes key indicators of BFS firms' productivity and process health. To measure and visually represent a firm's key performance indicators (KPIs), LSS offers techniques such as Gauge R-R, process capability studies, and visual management. For example, visual management (or control) is an LSS technique employed where information is communicated by using visual signals instead of texts or other written

instructions. The design is deliberate in allowing quick recognition of the information being communicated in order to increase efficiency and clarity.
- LSS concepts help to balance logical thinking (for measurement and analysis) and intuitive thinking (for ideation). This makes the methodology most suitable for BFS. Logic is a way of using a set of concrete rules and formulas learned over time to come up with a decision. Several LSS tools like hypothesis testing, control charts enable this process. Intuition on the other hand is a way of using abstract information you have received from different aspects of life to create a sensible reasoning to come up with a decision. Tools like brainstorming, ideation matrix, Pugh matrix of LSS are predominantly intuition-based tools that enable finding solutions in improve/design phase of the LSS projects.
- LSS projects help BFS organizations to monitor process performance using control charts and sustain their results over time with robust controls and mistake-proofing (poka-yoke) concepts, including automations. The control chart is a graph used to study how a process changes over time. It has a central line for the average, an upper line for the upper control limit, and a lower line for the lower control limit. These lines determined from historical data are used to compare current data to these lines and to draw conclusions about whether the process variation is in control or not.

However, LSS deployments in BFS are to be handled with sensitivity given the higher risk in the firms, due to their direct and almost complete reliance on customers' funds.

3.3 Understanding Key Performance Indicators in Banks for Deriving LSS Opportunities

For improving quality excellence, banks need the underlying capabilities that enable them to progress consistently. These include process performance, complexity management, and continuous improvement and collaboration between front and back offices. Among these, process performance management is the most important and critical element of the bank, which highlights the process complexities leading to continuous improvement and thus creating a culture of collaboration. Hence, key performance indicators (KPIs) become important. According to FinPa New Media, KPIs are defined as quantitative and qualitative measures used to review an organization's progress against its goals. These are broken down and set as targets for achievement by departments and individuals. The achievement of these targets is reviewed at regular intervals (FinPa New Media 2009). KPIs, in the EFQM excellence model, are defined as "What the organization is achieving in relation to its planned performance." Essentially, "the results document the relationship between what organizations do in terms of quality management practices and the results they achieve in several types of outcomes (NIST 2010)." The starting point for choosing which performance indicators are a key to a particular company should be those that the board uses to manage the business. In the banking industry, few of the KPI include customer retention, customer penetration, asset quality, capital adequacy, assets under management, loan loss, etc. Traditionally, a common metric used to measure performance has been net income. According to a study conducted by PwC in 2011, this metric does not totally serve the purpose of measuring how effectively a bank is functioning in relation to its size and does not truly reflect its asset efficiency. Another important KPI used often in the banking industry is net promoter score (NPS). It is important to consider other KPI in order to measure a retail bank's performance. Current ratio, working capital, returns on equity, debt to equity ratio, net profit margin, inventory turnover, accounts receivable turnover is few of the critical metrics. Several studies highlighted the importance of KPIs in retail banking setup. A few banks use a next-product-to-buy (NPTB) model to assist a retail bank with identifying the customer KPIs who were likely to purchase a specific loan product. Devising standards and metrics for measuring the customer loyalty in retail banks have been another challenge. Banks have limited their loyalty KPIs to product-specific programs or simple date-based recognition programs. From the back-office banking operations perspective, most of the KPIs get established in service-level agreements (SLA). With the globalization and increase in the business process outsourcing opportunities in the banking industry, the documentation of KPI as part of SLA has increased. SLAs commonly include segments to address: a definition of services, performance measurement, problem management, customer duties, warranties and disaster recovery features (Source: http://www.sla-zone.co.uk/).

Delivering a defect-free accurate output to the customers without compromising on the turnaround time of delivery becomes critical for the banking back offices (Sunder and Antony 2015). Measuring data and process performance are an essential element for any organization. This becomes specifically important for banks as they maintain huge databases of customer confidential information and all processes deal with involving money transactions. The KPI measurement provides a direction to the bank, highlighting the areas for improvement. The quality levels of the bank cannot be improved by merely measuring KPIs. This is where the CI methodologies like LSS help in improving the KPI levels as per the defined customer conformance standards. Hence, it becomes a prerequisite for any organization to mature as a metric-based organization in order to imbibe any quality methodology for process improvements.

References

Arnold M (2018) How US banks took over the financial world. Financial Times, Sept 16, 2018. https://www.ft.com/content/6d9ba066-9eee-11e8-85da-eeb7a9ce36e4.
Lessambo, F. I. (2020). *The US banking system*. Berlin: Springer.

NIST. (2010). National institute of standards and technology: The 2009–2010 criteria for performance excellence (MBNQA) [Online]. Available at www.nist.gov/baldrige/publications/criteria.cfm

Sunder, M. V., & Antony, J. (2015). Six-sigma for improving top-box customer satisfaction score for a banking call centre. *Production Planning and Control, 26*(16), 1291–1305.

4. Lean Six Sigma for Services—A Morphological Analysis of Research Literature

This chapter presents a morphological analysis of research literature on LSS for services. This chapter was conceived further to publication of an article entitled "A morphological analysis of research literature on Lean Six Sigma for services" appeared in the *International Journal of Operations & Production Management* (Sunder M 2018). The systematic literature review presented here through the MA technique provides directions for future research on this topic. A total of 355 research gaps are identified as an outcome of this exercise. Figure 4.1 presents a concept map of this chapter.

4.1 An Overview of Lean Six Sigma in Services

The integration of Lean with Six Sigma could add to the synergies in organizational processes, especially in the services sector. For example, Hines et al. (2004) indicated that it is possible to integrate Lean with other approaches, without contradicting its objective of providing customers with value. Lean combined with Six Sigma balances employee empowerment (both top-down and bottom-up) and creates synergies for process improvements. Six Sigma without Lean would only involve a cache of tools for improvement, but without strategy or structure to drive the system. LSS delivers better results than either Lean or Six Sigma applied in isolation.

George (2002) in his book *Lean Six Sigma: Combining Six Sigma Quality with Lean Speed* introduced the term "LSS." Though it is possible that the term LSS has been used even before, there is no concrete evidence found in the literature till 2002. A year later, another book—Lean Six Sigma for services—justified the applicability of LSS in services (George 2003). The claim that Lean and Six Sigma have a complementary relationship is widely accepted today in the corporate world. LSS has gained immense popularity in recent years due to the powerful synergy resulting from integrating Lean and Six Sigma practices. Being a hybrid

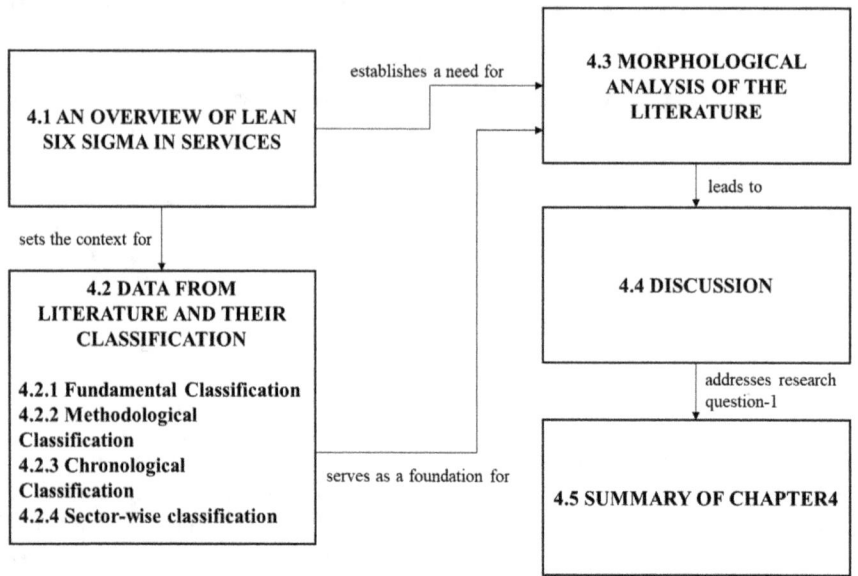

Fig. 4.1 Concept map of this chapter

methodology, LSS overcomes the shortcomings of Lean by also helping reduce process variations and defects, leading to higher customer satisfaction and bottom-line benefits to firms. LSS is widely used to transform separate, functionally reactive service organizations into cross-functional, learning organizations. A recent global study, conducted among 85 LSS professionals across different service organizations, revealed that 98.8% of the respondents preferred LSS over using Lean or Six Sigma separately for process improvements (Sunder M 2013). Today, more than 70% of Fortune 500 companies across various services recognize LSS' value. However, LSS for services, as an approach to CI, is yet to fully mature into a specific area of academic research.

4.2 Data from Literature and Their Classification

Research literature on LSS employed in services published in relevant journals—both, academic and practitioner—with a focus on quality management have been collected for the review. As a part of the systematic literature review (Tranfield et al. 2003), an online literature search was performed for publications from 2003 to 2015. This revealed a comprehensive set of papers on LSS. However, it is possible that a few papers that were unintentionally not investigated as a part of this study may exist. A five-stage protocol used for systematic identification and scoping of papers is featured below.

4.2 Data from Literature and Their Classification

1. A search was conducted in the "Abstract" field of the following databases—Emerald, Taylor and Francis, Springer, IEEE Xplore, Mendeley, Science Direct, Wiley, Elsevier, Sage, INFORMS, Inderscience, ASQ and HBR, with the search terms: "Lean Six Sigma," "LSS" and "Lean Six Sigma for Services" for the period from 2003 to 2015. This resulted in a total of 803 relevant articles. Various related combinations of keywords only led to subsets of these 803 articles.
2. The duplicate results were eliminated using the Mendeley desktop software. This led to a reduced number of 653 articles.
3. A large number of articles dealing exclusively with the manufacturing sector were excluded. Then, reading through the abstracts, 416 articles relevant to services were identified.
4. From among them, 136 articles published in journals listed in Scopus or ABS Academic Journal Quality Guide 2015 were identified.
5. A mechanical search of review articles should be supplemented by an organic search to obtain comprehensive search output. Hence, an organic search was performed to identify other relevant papers that were cited in these 136 articles. This search brought the final total to 175 articles, spread across 67 journals.

4.2.1 Fundamental Classification of LSS Research

More than 100 authors have contributed to the body of knowledge through 175 papers in 67 journals. Significant contributors include (and are not limited to) Antony J., Douglas A., Dahlgaard-Park S.M., Bendell T., Sarkar A., Chiarini A., Ghosh S., Kumar M., and Laureani A. The classification framework reveals that the contributors are from 26 different countries. The contributions from the USA, the UK, India, Sweden, the Netherlands, Italy, and Australia constitute 80% of the publications. This classification also reveals that 6 out of 67 journals contributed to 50% of the overall publications on the subject. They are *International Journal of Lean Six Sigma (34 papers), Total Quality Management and Business Excellence (16), International Journal of Quality and Reliability Management (14), The TQM Journal (14), International Journal of Productivity and Performance Management (11) and Quality Progress (5)*.

4.2.2 Methodological Classification of LSS Research

Table 4.1 presents an overview of the research methods, sources of data, proportion of papers using specific methodologies and sample papers. In all, 30 theoretical papers and 145 empirical studies appeared. The theoretical publications included conceptual or desk analysis by various researchers. The empirical papers were limited to descriptive and experimental studies that have been further classified based on data collection methods. A total of 93 papers appeared to have used

Table 4.1 Methodological classification of reviewed papers

				No. of papers	% Papers
Research method	Theoretical			30	17
	Empirical	Primary data	Case study/action research	66	38
			Questionnaire	12	7
			Interviews	8	5
			Viewpoints	5	3
			Experiment data	2	1
		Secondary data		24	14
		Mixed methods		28	16

primary data collection methods. The primary data category consisted of 66 papers dominated by case studies and action research. This category also included questionnaire methods, interviews, viewpoints and experiment data sources used in the remaining 27 papers. Thus, we can observe that there is a need for more empirical research. There were only 24 papers that leveraged secondary data from existing literature and public data sources. The use of multiple primary research methods (mixed methods) was identified in 28 of the reviewed papers.

4.2.3 Chronological Classification of LSS Research

TQM was recognized as the most widespread quality management approach from the beginning of the 1990s. However, during the first decade of the new millennium, emerging PI methodologies such as Lean and Six Sigma seem to have overtaken TQM. The proven success of Lean and Six Sigma individually helped LSS to be recognized by practitioners and academicians as a powerful CI methodology for customer satisfaction. Hence, researchers have tacitly accepted LSS as a CI methodology. From the early 2000s, the evolution of LSS has been significant. Though LSS for services was introduced as a concept in 2003, there were no specific papers from the reviewed literature on the topic till 2004.

2004–2007: During this period, new quality techniques for CI were adopted. These were beyond the earlier quality philosophies like TQM. The papers focused on the modern quality movement and called Lean and Six Sigma as structured PI techniques in the new age of high technology. The need for upgrading the skills and knowledge of CI professionals through LSS toolkits for effective quality management was identified. Though researchers appreciated Lean and Six Sigma as distinct CI methodologies, they also noticed a linkage between the two. Strengths and weaknesses of Lean and Six Sigma were assessed to identify common and distinct features of the two methodologies leading to several exploratory and descriptive studies for integration. With this, the focus shifted toward understanding LSS as a single hybrid methodology rather than as being made of individual CI programs in isolation. Several case studies and action research papers highlighted the integrated LSS approach for CI. The practical implications tinted the importance of data measurement, leadership, organization culture, innovation, customer focus, fact-based approach, agility, focus on results and project management in the context of successful LSS implementation for services. However, the integrated LSS methodology received some criticism.

2008–2011: This period witnessed a synergy of LSS implementation in services. It was reported that the overall popularity of LSS had been growing in services, specifically in healthcare services. Researchers confirmed that LSS is not merely an integration of Lean and Six Sigma, rather a management strategy which can deliver significant benefits much higher than Lean or Six Sigma individually. A few scholars demonstrated that LSS practitioners in contemporary organizations have the responsibility to lead quality at the strategic level. Others claimed that LSS certification practice is important to determine the competency level of the practitioners. Other authors identified LSS certification standards to be used in organizations, drawing on the best practices from major companies. Researchers felt a need for structured application of LSS, and hence, several frameworks emerged. Publications also identified several critical success factors (CSFs) which could lead to the success of LSS. A few authors have discussed the implementation issues of LSS. For example, it was argued that all processes cannot be taken up simultaneously for CI, and hence, project selection becomes a key implementation issue. de Koning et al. (2010) identified seven standard LSS project definition templates, which have explicitly stated goals and a solid business rationale for project management. Hoerl and Gardner (2010) claimed that LSS promoted creativity and innovation. They acknowledged that LSS was the best approach for addressing major "solution unknown" problems. From the reviewed papers, 23 case studies were identified between 2008 and 2011, showcasing the successful application of LSS in various services sectors (presented in sector-wise classification). As the success of LSS caught fire across services, there have been questions from critics about the assessment methods. It was also argued that LSS implementations should have a realistic evaluation by which assessing and considering the individual characteristics of an organization's social environment could lead to successful CI. An early assessment model for LSS was suggested by Corbett (2011) based on six attributes—leadership, strategic planning, customer and market focus, measurement, analysis and knowledge management, employee focus and process management.

2012–2015: During this period, management thinkers highlighted the importance of LSS in the context of quality management and claimed that the focus had shifted from being initially on TQM to tools and techniques, and then to core values needed for building a quality and business excellence culture. A few authors argued that LSS as a management strategy of services firms was often built to create a specific quality profile, which they retained over time. In addition to the debate surrounding LSS as a management strategy, the body of literature on dynamic capabilities (DCs) is also of particular interest to researchers. McAdam et al. (2014)

identified LSS as a best practice as a part of their research on performance measurement models, since it helped improve operational measures for greater process capabilities. Various studies highlighted the implementation of LSS in new services like services supply chain, higher education, hospitality. Several other authors noticed LSS as a differentiating factor when integrated with other quality philosophies in the services context for CI, due to its success and popularity. According to Bhamu and Sangwan (2014), a structured cross-fertilization of LSS methodology can be used in a wide range of projects to tackle specific problems. Adding to the previous researchers, several other CSFs were identified which included readiness factors and critical failure factors. Others argued that the traditional LSS methodology needs to be customized based on the nature of services for changing environments. With sector-specific customization in LSS methodology, several new frameworks emerged during this period. Contributions on customizing LSS toolkits were also witnessed during this period. Global studies about the implementation of LSS found it fit for services in human resources management. Challenges faced in implementing LSS in pure services environments were also identified. A total of 37 case studies and action research papers were published on various services in organizations.

4.2.4 Sector-Wise Classification of LSS Research

The review found that 9% publications (16 papers) appeared from services in the manufacturing sector and 43% (76 papers) of the publications were found to be generic across the services sector. Examples of services in manufacturing include hiring processes, logistics, packaging of goods, safety, administrative processes. These publications included LSS concepts, frameworks, theoretical contributions and exploratory and descriptive studies applicable across all services. The remaining 83 papers were sector specific and spread across the services sector.

The highest contributions appeared in health care, followed by education, and 6 out of 7 papers presented case studies on banking, financial services, and insurance. Reduction in costs, risks, defects, and process-times and improvement in customer satisfaction, employee satisfaction, process quality, cultural transformation, and business value were LSS' proven benefits stated in these papers.

The recent publications of LSS in non-profit organizations clarify that it not only helps organizations deliver bottom-line benefits, but also helps transform organizational culture for business value and excellence. Consolidating this discussion with the case studies published in education, it is evident that LSS not only contributes to CI and cultural transformation in business enterprises but also in social enterprises where defining the "customer" is unclear (Holmes et al. 2005).

4.3 Morphological Analysis of the Literature

Morphological analysis (MA) is an analytical technique to be used with grounded creativity for investigating and structuring the total set of relationships contained in multi-dimensional, non-quantifiable contexts to eliminate vagueness. It involves examining the entire set of combinations of possible values of various dimensions of a concept (Zwicky 1969) to identify the gaps. It provides a method to identify and investigate elements of a system (or a concept) in its existing form and to explore possible configurations (or opportunities) which the system could have. Using this method, the entire set of unstructured concepts is put into a framework, defined by (a) a set of dimensions representing the ontological structural components of the concept being studied, and (b) "variants" representing the extant as well as possible ontological manifestations corresponding to each of the dimensions. All of the variant values in the morphological field are compared with one another in the manner of a cross-relationships matrix. Here, each variant pair is examined, a judgment is made as to whether, or to what extent the pair can coexist, i.e., represent a consistent relationship. There is no reference to direction or causality, but only to mutual and logical consistency. Using this matrix, a typical morphological field can be reduced depending on the logic relevant to the context of the problem structure.

It is important to note that the development of an MA framework demands judgement, and it is quite likely that different authors may develop different MA frameworks even from the same data set they use to represent the same unstructured concept. However, the aggregated contents of all such MA frameworks will theoretically be the same, although the form of representations could vary. This indicates the objectivity of the approach toward theory building through an ST perspective.

4.3.1 Dimension 1: Organizational Context of Application

Porter (2011), in his book on competitive advantage, described a chain of activities common to all businesses and divided them into five primary and four support activities. Later, many researchers endorsed this classification of the organizational value chain for further studies. Here, these activities are used to analyze, in an organizational context, the applications of LSS presented in the reviewed literature and place them in the MA framework. Hence, the variables defined under this dimension are as per Porter's classification of an organizational value chain.

Primary activities:

- Variant 1 Inbound logistics: involves relationships with suppliers and include all the activities required to receive, store, and disseminate inputs and related information.

- Variant 2 Operations: are all the activities required to transform inputs into outputs through value addition (in the context of services).
- Variant 3 Outbound logistics: includes all the activities required to collect, store and distribute the output, and related information.
- Variant 4 Marketing and sales: activities that inform buyers about products and services, induce the buyers to purchase them and facilitate their purchase.
- Variant 5 Post-sale services: includes all the activities required to keep the products or services working effectively for the buyer after they are sold and delivered.

Support activities:

- Variant 6 Procurement: the acquisition of inputs, or resources, for the firm, and the related information.
- Variant 7 Human resource management: consists of all activities involved in recruiting, hiring, training, developing, compensating and laying off personnel.
- Variant 8 Technology: pertains to the equipment, hardware, software, procedures, and technical knowledge used by the firm to transform inputs into outputs.
- Variant 9 Infrastructure: serves the company's needs and ties its various parts together, and it consists of functions or departments such as accounting, legal, finance, planning, public affairs, government relations, quality assurance, and general management.

4.3.2 Dimension 2: Desired Outcomes

This dimension elaborates the desired outcomes through the application of LSS in services. From the literature, eight short-term/transactional outcomes and six long-term/strategic outcomes have been identified. These are basically the key tangible and intangible metrics which LSS could potentially improve or enable in the services context.

Short-term/transactional tangible outcomes:

- Variant 10 Cycle time and cost reduction: time taken to complete the defined tasks and subsequently reducing the cost involved in the associated resources consumed.
- Variant 11 Increase in revenue: increase in sales or acquisition of new customers, new business, new markets and thereby increasing the revenue
- Variant 12 Risk management: both preventive and corrective actions toward risk reduction with appropriate controls
- Variant 13 Quality, efficiency, and productivity improvement: quality improvement across different levels of the value chain, efficiency improvement and productive work

4.3 Morphological Analysis of the Literature

- Variant 14 Customer or employee satisfaction: under the broad category of stakeholders' management
- Variant 15 Rework and error reduction: redundancy, number of defects and associated rework involved in correcting them.

Short-term/transactional intangible outcomes:

- Variant 16 Enabler for effective decision-making environment.
- Variant 17 Enabler for incremental innovation and CI mind-set.

Long-term/strategic tangible outcomes:

- Variant 18 Improved competitiveness/market share.
- Variant 19 Enabler for breakthrough and disruptive innovation.
- Variant 20 Knowledge management: effective management of knowledge in the organization including knowledge creation, knowledge sharing, and knowledge dissipation.

Long-term/strategic intangible outcomes:

- Variant 21 Learning capability: capability of an organization to learn from its environment.
- Variant 22 Business excellence capability: capability of an organization to excel what has been learnt.
- Variant 23 Dynamic capability: refers to the capability of an organization to adapt quickly to independently changing environments, or to even influence its environment, for creating a competitive edge that would be difficult for others to imitate.

4.3.3 Dimension 3: Implementation Systems

This dimension maps the substantive approaches, types of resources used in implementation, and various implementation issues discussed in the reviewed papers.

Substantive approaches:

- Variant 24 Six Sigma followed by Lean.
- Variant 25 Lean Six Sigma as a hybrid methodology.
- Variant 26 Lean and Six Sigma in parallel.

Resources for implementation:

- Variant 27 Operational human resources: front-line staff, mid-managers
- Variant 28 Financial: allotted money, capital, cash, and associated budget
- Variant 29 Leadership human resources: senior management personnel

Implementation issues:

- Variant 30 Readiness factors: the factors that determine the readiness level of the firm before embarking on the implementation
- Variant 31 Challenges: bottlenecks during implementation
- Variant 32 Success/failure factors: the key success or failure factors presence or absence of which (respectively) leads to not meeting the intended purpose of the implementation

4.3.4 Dimension 4: LSS Tools and Techniques

This dimension maps the LSS tools which are predominantly preferred for usage/application identified, from the reviewed papers:

- Variant 33 Graphical/non-statistical tools: tools used to visually depict the results
- Variant 34 Statistical tools: tools used to clarify the statistical significance.

4.3.5 Dimension 5: Integration with Other Philosophies

This dimension elaborates upon the application of LSS as an integrative methodology with other philosophies relevant to services:

- Variant 35 Quality management philosophies and other organizational practices.
- Variant 36 Systems thinking concepts: associated concepts dealing with the ST
- Variant 37 Innovation practices: practices that promote, trigger, manage or educate about innovation

4.3.6 Dimension 6: Evaluation Methods

The reviewed papers reveal that there are different types of evaluation methods, adapted in organizational contexts for assessing the success of LSS. These are grouped below:

4.3 Morphological Analysis of the Literature

- Variant 38 Milestone-based: success of LSS evaluated based on percent deployment across organization.
- Variant 39 Function-based: evaluation of LSS implementation based on functional deployment.
- Variant 40 Project-based: evaluation of LSS implementation based on project by project deployment.

4.4 Discussion

It is evident that the literature reviewed here has enabled the mapping of 9 variants under the organizational context of applications, 14 variants under desired outcomes, 9 variants under implementation systems, 2 variants under tools and techniques, 3 variables under integration with other philosophies, and 3 variables under evaluation methods. This leads to 20,412 ($9 \times 14 \times 9 \times 2 \times 3 \times 3$) combinatorial configurations across the six dimensions. As a next step in the analysis–synthesis process, combinatorial relationships between the variables associated within a dimension were removed to eliminate the internal combinations. For example, meaningful combinations for further research cannot be realized between the pair inbound logistics and outbound logistics. Similarly, the graphical tools–statistical tools pair also does not yield meaningful combinations that can be probed further. These are separate pairs of variables under the same dimension.

This process results in the refined Concurrent Research Analysis Matrix showed in Fig. 4.1, where all the dimensional values in the MA framework are compared pairwise with one another. During this process, there was no reference to direction or causality, but only the relational consistency between the paired variables was analyzed. This resulted in 355 research gaps, which could be considered as possible opportunities for future research. However, researchers should apply appropriate judgement for direction and causality, before selecting a research gap for focused research. The respective pairs of factors which reveal research gaps should be examined; and then, a selection judgment has to be made based on whether and to what extent the pairs can coexist to represent a meaningful relationship deserving focused research. The novelty of this review is to point to both academicians and practitioners, focused directions on research opportunities and questions to ponder on the subject "LSS for Services," for future research/study (Fig. 4.2).

A few of the broad areas are highlighted below:

- Application and comparison of LSS methodology in various distinct service sub-sectors, namely, LSS in health care, LSS in education, LSS in banking, and financial services, etc.

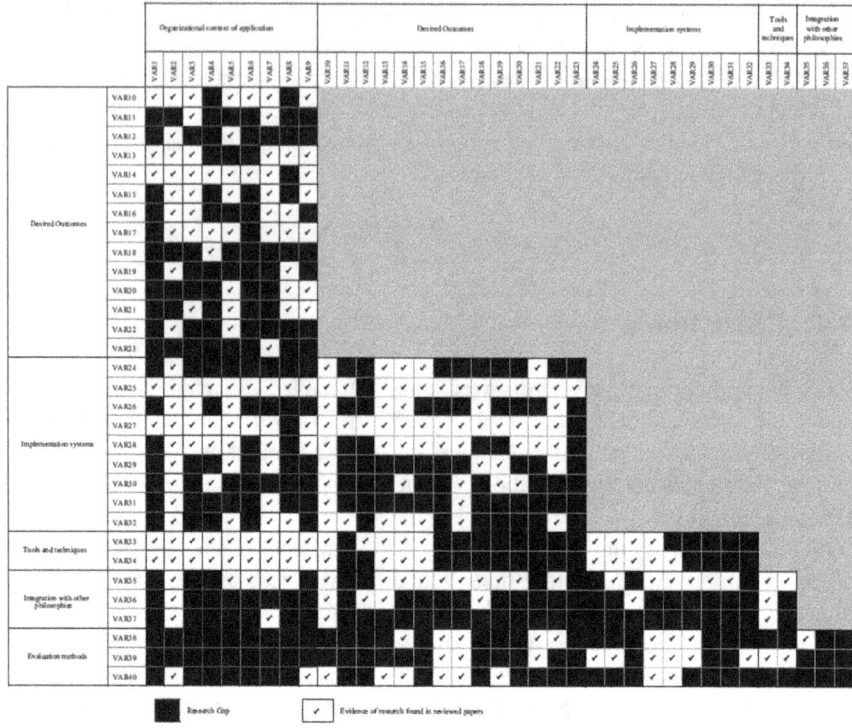

Fig. 4.2 Concurrent research analysis matrix

- Customization in models of LSS methodology deployment in organizational contexts, namely, customization of LSS deployment in inbound logistics, outbound logistics, post-sale services, etc.
- To validate the hypothesis that LSS is an enabler of incremental innovation and continuous improvement mindsets in service organizations.
- Validation of various tangible and intangible outcomes of LSS (defined above) in each of the services sub-sectors.
- Impact of LSS deployment on competitiveness and market share in services (specific to each service sub-sector).
- To validate the hypothesis that LSS is an enabler for breakthrough and disruptive innovation in service organizations (specific to each service sub-sector).
- Synergies of LSS and knowledge management and the impacts, specific to each service sub-sector.
- To validate if LSS deployment in services firms could contribute to customer as well as employee satisfaction. If so, what would be the attributes, influencing factors, and measures of success?
- "Impact of" and "impact on" human resources due to various tangible outcomes of LSS deployment in services.

- Utilization of financial resources for deploying LSS across primary and support processes in services and its impact on the organization.
- Is LSS an enabler of learning capability in service firms?
- Can LSS be a dynamic capability in firms?
- Customization of LSS toolkit for services sector (applicability, ease of use, preferred usage at various primary and support functions in each of the defined service sectors).
- Synergies of LSS and other quality management practices in services (e.g., LSS and ISO, LSS and balanced scorecard, for each of the services sectors).
- Integration of LSS with systems thinking concepts and innovation practices (specific to each service sector).
- How to evaluate the success of LSS deployment in services? (conceptual models, preferred usage and validation for each service sector).

References

Bhamu, J., & Singh Sangwan, K. (2014). Lean manufacturing: Literature review and research issues. *International Journal of Operations and Production Management, 34*(7), 876–940.

Corbett, L. M. (2011). Lean Six Sigma: The contribution to business excellence. *International Journal of Lean Six Sigma, 2*(2), 118–131.

de Koning, H., Does, R. J., Groen, A., & Kemper, B. P. (2010). Generic Lean Six Sigma project definitions in publishing. *International Journal of Lean Six Sigma, 1*(1), 39–55.

George, M. L. (2002). *Lean six sigma: Combining six sigma quality with lean speed/Michael L.* USA: George. McGraw-Hill.

George, M. L. (2003). *How to use lean speed and six sigma quality to improve services and transactions.*

Hines, P., Holweg, M., & Rich, N. (2004). Learning to evolve: A review of contemporary lean thinking. *International journal of operations and production management, 24*(10), 994–1011.

Hoerl, R. W., & Gardner, M. M. (2010). Lean Six Sigma, creativity, and innovation. *International Journal of Lean Six Sigma, 1*(1), 30–38.

Holmes, M. C., Kumar, A., & Jenicke, L. O. (2005). Improving the effectiveness of the academic delivery process utilizing Six Sigma. *Issues in Information Systems, 2*(1), 353–359.

McAdam, R., Hazlett, S. A., & Galbraith, B. (2014). The role of performance measurement models in multi level alignment: An exploratory case analysis in the utilities sector. *International Journal of Operations and Production Management, 34*(9), 1153–1183.

Porter, M. E. (2011). *Competitive advantage of nations: Creating and sustaining superior performance.* New York, NY: Simon and Schuster.

Sunder, M. V. (2013). Synergies of Lean Six Sigma. *IUP Journal of Operations Management, 12*(1), 21.

Sunder M, V., Ganesh, L. S., & Marathe, R. R. (2018). A morphological analysis of research literature on Lean Six Sigma for services. *International Journal of Operations & Production Management, 38*(1), 149–182.https://doi.org/10.1108/IJOPM-05-2016-0273.

Tranfield, D., Denyer, D., & Smart, P. (2003). Towards a methodology for developing evidence-informed management knowledge by means of systematic review. *British Journal of Management, 14*(3), 207–222.

Zwicky, F. (1969). *Discovery, invention, research through the morphological approach.*

5. Lean Six Sigma Projects in Banking Firms—Implementation Cases

This chapter presents a discussion of the analysis of LSS project implementations in banks. This chapter was conceived further to the publication of two articles entitled —(Sunder M et al. 2019) "Lean Six Sigma in consumer banking—an empirical inquiry" appeared in the *International Journal of Quality & Reliability Management* and (Sunder M 2016) "Rejects reduction in a retail bank using Lean Six Sigma" appeared in *Production Planning & Control* Journal. The lessons learned, and their implications are presented here following the analysis of the two cases accompanied by observations of and reflections upon the practices.

5.1 An Overview of Research Literature on LSS in Banking

Published academic research concerning the applicability of LSS in BFS is apparently limited to only five refereed papers in total (Peteros and Maleyeff 2015; Lokkerbol et al. 2012; Wang and Chen 2010; Delgado et al. 2010; Koning and Does 2008), and none of these are specific to the consumer banking context. Peteros (2015) used LSS along with consumption mapping concepts to develop a methodology for standardization of self-directed investors to avoid adverse decision behaviors. Lokkerbol et al. (2012) devised a case-based approach to identify eight generic project definition templates used to identify project opportunities in BFS firms. Wang and Chen (2010) observed methods to integrate TRIZ with LSS in the context of banking services. Delgado et al. (2010) performed a longitudinal study in a financial organization collecting 10 years' data to highlight benefits derived from LSS implementation, such as lowering the operational costs, improving processes and product quality, increased efficiency, which leads to the increase of productivity, agility and versatility. Similarly, Koning and Does (2008) demonstrated the importance of incremental innovations through LSS by studying four case studies from Dutch multinational insurance companies. An overview of these papers reveals some interesting concepts toward organizational implementation of LSS for operational benefits. However, these studies did not speak much about the real-time implementation of LSS projects in a banking setup. Further, these studies are scoped either generic to the BFS sector or oriented toward financial interfaces like insurance companies.

5.2 Evidence from Practitioners' Literature

Due to the very limited academic research, practitioner literature was examined through online sources that revealed some interesting evidence of the applicability and success of LSS in consumer banks. An overview of the same is presented below:

- According to Hoffman (2006), the online banking team at the Bank of America used LSS projects to improve desktop authentication techniques and introduce live text chat for improving customer support.
- The LSS team at HSBC transformed an underperforming unit in the banking division with the DMAIC approach. They used tools such as process mapping and data partitioning. The result was a 274% improvement in net income and a culture of CI (Dan 2004).
- A case study on the Standard Bank Group has highlighted their use of LSS methods for project management to reduce waste and errors in transaction processing (Woods 2010a, b). As a result of these improvements, the bank realized aggregate savings of $64.84 million in a period of four years.
- Westpac, an Australian consumer financial services firm, launched its LSS program in IT services to reduce redundant banking processes. To help accomplish these goals, Westpac expanded their LSS training efforts over 600 frontline and operations employees (Woods 2010a, b).
- Bank of Montreal embarked upon their LSS journey in 2005. Since then, the bank has reduced errors, improved cycle time, and eliminated waste. They had anticipated annualized savings of nearly $55 million over a five-year benefit (Online Source 2012).

5.3 Real-Time Applications of LSS in Banking

According to Eisenhardt (1989), reflection and comparison with existing theory in real-time settings can help in bringing objectivity to the research process. This approach encourages reflective, practitioner-based insights and inputs which could reveal both the challenges and outcomes of the investigation. According to Yin (2003), the case study method is used to illuminate a particular situation by means of gaining a close in-depth understanding of it. It helps in making direct, real-time observations, collects data, and analyzes prevailing situations and settings, compared to merely relying on the derived data. Empirical exploratory research is appropriate to understand the application of LSS in real-time banking environments, as very little is known in the academic literature about LSS in BFS, unlike its implementation in other services.

The case study approach allows a more direct comparison between the similarities and differences of the implementation practices in two or more different contexts. It can help create more robust and testable theories than those based on single cases. However, each single case is of equal importance even when multiple cases are studied. When the multi-case study approach is adopted, the individual cases, which share a common characteristic or exhibit a common phenomenon, are categorically bound together to make conclusions. Though strong generic conclusions cannot be arrived at by one such study, one can use the multi-case study approach as a step toward theory building.

5.3.1 Approach to LSS Project Management

A three-stage approach is followed. In Stage-1, appropriate candidates for the study were selected. This includes identification of (a) the consumer banks where LSS projects could be undertaken and (b) readiness assessment in the identified banks. In Stage-2, LSS project opportunities were identified in the banks through stakeholder engagement. Finally, in Stage-3, LSS projects were executed.

- *Stage 1: Engagement*: A proposal letter was drafted to conduct LSS projects, detailing the scope, benefits and potential success of LSS in service organizations. The proposal highlighted the success of LSS deployment in BFS organizations gathered via online practitioner literature. Permission to undertake LSS projects for operational process improvements was sought via e-mail from the heads of operations of six global consumer banking offshore centers of multinational banks located in India. Three among the six banks responded to the proposal for initial discussions. Conversational interviews were conducted with the top-management personnel of the bank and further coded with an aim to perform the readiness checks. The purpose of this engagement was to understand the factors suggested by George (2002):

  - Experiences with change initiatives from the past
  - Understanding of corporate strategy and priorities
  - Current attitude toward LSS
  - How decisions are made, how conflict is resolved
  - How work gets done (collaboration vs. silos)
  - Openness to new approaches and appetite for process improvements.

- *Stage 2: Opportunity Identification*: Based on the understanding of Stage-1, two different approaches were used to identify the LSS project opportunities. In Cases A and B, since the target stakeholder group comprised only limited managers, joint interviews were conducted and further coded to capture the voice of the customers (VOC) to identify an appropriate LSS project opportunity. In Case C, since there were multiple client groups involved in decision making and since the bank followed a matrix organization structure, 46 management stakeholders were involved. They had multiple concerns and client escalations for PI. Hence, in Case C, a questionnaire (based on the Kano model, developed by Professor Noriaki Kano in the 1980s) was adopted to identify the LSS project opportunity.

- **Stage 3: Execution**: LSS DMAIC methodology was used to execute the selected project opportunities. The projects were executed over a period of 6–8 months (each), including the "Control" phase where improvements were monitored. The formal closure of the projects was signed-off by the respective top-management personnel after acknowledging the tangible business benefits.

5.3.2 LSS Project Management Method Used

The DMAIC problem-solving methodology of LSS was used as it could catalyze Six Sigma and Lean tools at the appropriate project management stages (George 2002). The DMAIC methodology is most effective for the implementation of LSS for PI in organizational contexts. Literature shows evidence that LSS DMAIC is the most successful methodology for PI in the services sector and could hence be considered as appropriate even for BFS. Accordingly, the main phases of the DMAIC methodology are:

1. **Define**: This phase deals with collecting the VOC by means of surveys, interviews, etc., followed by drafting the project charter. Project metrics for improvement are identified in this phase along with validation of the LSS project charter with the project champion, viz. the management representative who will be involved in providing production-level governance to the project.
2. **Measure**: This phase deals with collecting data and mapping the process, assessing the measurement system, and calculating the process capability. Baseline data collection plan, normality testing, control charts, defects per million opportunities (DPMO) calculation or parts per million (PPM) calculation with Cpk and Ppk values, and Gauge R-R are a few of the LSS tools used in this phase.
3. **Analyze**: This phase deals with identifying the root causes of the problem. Alongside the project manager, process analysts (subject matter experts) from operations play an important role in this phase. Brainstorming, data collection for causes, Pareto analysis, hypothesis testing, Gemba, value-stream mapping, fishbone diagram, and 5-Why analysis are a few of the LSS tools used in this phase.
4. **Improve**: This phase deals with the identification of improvements, validation of the improvement plan with the stakeholders, obtaining budget approvals, and implementation of the process changes. Senior management, project champion,

and sponsors play a vital role in this phase. Brainstorming, Pugh matrix, benchmarking, and mistake-proofing are a few of the LSS tools used in this phase.
5. *Control*: This phase deals with placing the right controls for sustaining the improvements and documenting the lessons learned from the project. This phase also validates the PI contributions of the project with a data comparison of metric performance "before" and "after" the project. Control charts, control plan, and process capability study are a few of the tools used. Completion of this phase marks the closure of the LSS project.

5.4 Case Studies

Three case studies are presented below here, and the discussions provide details of the LSS steps followed. In all three cases (Sunder M et al. 2019; Sunder M 2016), the value contributed by the DMAIC phases toward realizing significant improvements in the project outcome metrics, the results, and their implications is also discussed.

5.4.1 Case A: Optimization of Employee Utilization

A case from the offshore transaction center of a multinational consumer bank, operating with 90 staff from India is presented below.

Define Phase: Intensive interviews were conducted with the bank's leadership team, process owners from the middle management, and frontline employees for capturing the VOC. This led to the identification of "*optimization of employee utilization in the bank's operations*" as the key requirement for the CI project. The employee utilization metric was found to explain the productivity of the process by looking at extra hours at work against the processed work volume on any particular day. A project charter (Fig. 5.1) was drafted to obtain the leadership team's consent for kick-starting the project. The project sponsor and champion were assigned from the leadership team to conduct periodic reviews and provide consistent governance. A project manager was assigned from a technical pool of LSS Black Belts. Baseline data of the employee utilization metric using the past six months' data revealed that the bank had been operating with 90 full-time employees (FTEs) between July 20XX and September 20XX, with an average utilization rate of 132%, leading to employee dissatisfaction and attrition. Hence, the project sought to optimize the utilization of around 100% within six months.

Measure Phase: To understand the processes in-scope and to capture time taken per activity, a process mapping activity was conducted alongside a time study. Highlights of the study were documented to identify elements contributing to the process complexity including decision boxes, number of handoffs, resource loading at process steps, and discrimination between value-added and non-value-added activities.

Project Charter	
Business case: The consumer banking operations consist of processes involved in account opening and maintenance units. The unit operates with 90 FTEs who process the client instructions. Owing to process stabilization, the client is now looking at productivity benefit initiatives as the next step to strengthen the business partnership.	**Project Team:** • Project manager: XXXX, LSS Black Belt • Project champion: XXXX, Function manager • Project sponsor: XXXX, Bank's director • Project support: from automation team, bank operational analysts and data management team members.
Problem statement: The bank is operating with 90 FTEs between July 20XX to September 20XX. Employee utilization was observed to be at 132%, leading to employee dissatisfaction and attrition. Hence, there is a need to optimize the utilization percentage through process improvements.	**Goal:** To improve the employee utilization percentage from 132% to 100% (~25% improvement) by February 20XX through appropriate productivity improvements in the process.
Project Metric: Employee utilization percentage = time spent by employees on work divided by the total time expected to be spent in office.	**Scope:** The project aims at optimizing the employee utilization rate for account opening and maintenance processes. All other processes including account closure, lien and share transfers are out of the scope of this project.

Fig. 5.1 Project charter

Metric baseline data was collected from July to September, and the metric performance was calculated by using the following formulae (operational definition of the metrics):

$$\text{Employee utilization} = \text{time spent by employees on work} / \text{total time expected to be spent in office}$$

$$\text{Time spent by employee on work} = \text{volumes processed by employee} \times \text{the standard time of work}$$

$$\text{Standard time of work} = \text{Average [time taken by staff on a particular transaction]}$$

On the metric data, normality–stability–capability tests are performed to understand the current as-is situation of the metric performance. An Anderson–Darling test was performed to check the normality, and the p value of the normality test was 0.552, confirming normality. The mean employee utilization was 131.9%, with a

5.4 Case Studies

standard deviation, "s" = 37.18%. The high standard deviation in the process justified the LSS project opportunity. Process stability for the utilization metric was analyzed using control charts. Because $s = 37.18\%$, the three-sigma control limits were far from the median. In the control chart, the "Lower Control Limit" = 17.21% and the "Upper Control Limit" = 246.7%. Though there were no special causes observed from the control chart, the variation due to common causes was relatively high.

For observing the process capability indices, the "Lower Specification Limit" (LSL) and "Upper Specification Limit" (USL) were set at 90% and 110%, respectively, in agreement with the project champion. Though the project target was to reduce employee utilization to 100%, lower employee utilization would lead to invoicing problems for the business. Hence, the LSL was set at 90%, indicating that utilization below 90% would be a defect. Hence, the optimization of the utilization percentage was set between 90 and 110%, and process performance outside these limits would constitute defects. The observed PPM showed that there were 825,688 defects observed in one million opportunities. The Cpk and Ppk values were close as rational sub-grouping of data would have been invalid due to the absence of batches. The high spread and the process being completely outside of the specification limits (Fig. 5.2) necessitated process improvement using the DMAIC method.

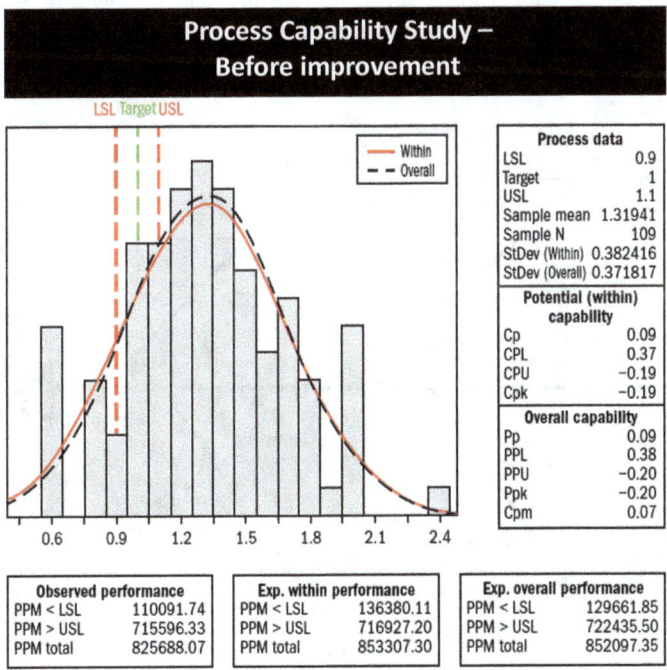

Fig. 5.2 Process capability of the baseline data

Analyze Phase: Multiple brainstorming sessions conducted to understand the reasons for excess employee utilization revealed multiple causes, which were grouped under four different causal streams using a fishbone diagram (Fig. 5.3). The list of causes collated was further validated to identify an unbiased vital-few root causes contributing to excess utilization of resources at the offshore center. This exercise was performed in three ways:

- Collecting sample data on the root causes and performing Pareto analysis and hypothesis testing wherever possible, and
- Gemba, or walking the floor to observe and validate the causes, and
- Performing value-stream mapping on specific process areas.

A data collection exercise was performed to collect data for the call reasons from branches and the branch locations. The data was analyzed using Pareto charts for identifying the root causes of the problem. Value-stream mapping was performed to understand the ad hoc request handling in the account maintenance and account opening processes. The analysis and opportunities for CI were highlighted (see Table 5.1).

Analysts were tested on their knowledge and skill levels. Process knowledge was evaluated on a scale of one to 10 (1 being "least proficient" and 10 "most proficient"). The impact of the knowledge-level of the analysts on the utilization metric was tested statistically. Since the knowledge-level data was found to be non-normal, the Kruskal–Wallis test was performed on the medians.

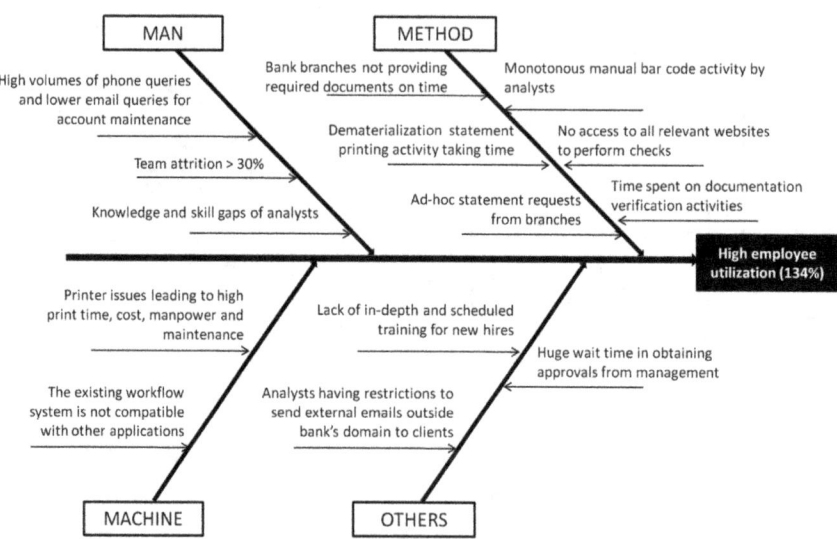

Fig. 5.3 Fishbone diagram of high employee utilization

5.4 Case Studies

Table 5.1 Data and process analysis

Cause	Analysis	Inference
High volumes of phone queries from branch offices for account maintenance	Pareto chart—reason for calls from branches	Vital-few reasons for branches to make phone calls were identified: • Clarification on discrepancies on the application form • Confirmation of execution questions • Booklet dispatch information • Pay-in instructions
Bank branches not providing required documents on time	[Pareto chart of approximate daily volumes by branch]	Pareto analysis showed that more follow-up, causing delays in obtaining coversheet is from: AMD, KANAK, BRAB, Fort Brokers, Baroda, FORT-MUM, NPT, MTRD, Vashi, SURAT and Pune
Time spent on ad hoc statement requests from branches	[Value-stream map: 35 branches, 25 requests/day, 15 minutes/request. File download from NSDL system → File transfer from NSDL to back-office system → Mail to branch. VAT: 0/0/2 minutes; NVAT: 2/26.33/0 minutes; Cycle time: 2 min / 26.33 min / 2 min]	Value-stream mapping was performed on ad hoc statement requests from branches' process, and the value-added ratio (VAR) only 4% of time spent on creating statements for branches
Time spent on the document verification	[Value-stream map: 35 branches; Application forms; CPA: G&S vendor; Citi APU team; DOCS check, PAN check, Other checks, Account opening, Archival to RMU (inc DRN forms). VAT: 0/0/15/11/0 minutes; NVAT: 2/15/15/19/0 minutes; Cycle time: 13/15/15/30/1,500 mins]	Value-stream mapping was performed on document verification process, and the VAR was only 6.9% of the total activities

(continued)

Table 5.1 (continued)

Cause	Analysis					Inference
	Knowledge	N	Median	Ave rank	Z	
Impact of analysts' Knowledge-level on team utilization	4	10	1.070	29.9	−0.40	Kruskal–Wallis test (non-normal data) confirmed there was no significant difference in the medians of the utilization levels across different knowledge-levels ($P > 0.05$). Hence, knowledge-level of the analysts is not a vital cause of the problem
	5	13	1.020	25.2	−1.50	
	6	6	1.140	28.7	−0.47	
	7	8	1.205	40.8	1.46	
	8	13	1.200	34.9	0.64	
	9	13	1.200	33.7	0.37	
	Overall	63		32.0		
	$H = 4.41$	DF = 5	**P = 0.492**			

Improve Phase: The project manager prepared an improvement plan by conducting brainstorming sessions with the project stakeholders' group. The improvements were governed by a team of three managers from the bank, after obtaining the project sponsor's consensus for implementation timelines and governance meetings. Communication e-mails were published daily as documented minutes of the meetings about what improvements had been achieved, what had been scheduled with timelines, and ownership details. This effective stakeholder management of appropriate involvement, influence and effective communication of information about PIs created a positive impact at the workplace. Employee morale and effective change management were boosted by involving the leadership team. Involving analysts in brainstorming helped in ownership assignment of CI. The following changes were implemented as a part of the project:

- *Reduction of over-processing waste*: Over-processing is one of the seven deadly wastes as per the Lean methodology. Second and third levels of inspection and quality assurance tasks on the transactions were eliminated. The project champion was hesitant to approve this improvement, as it was felt that eliminating inspection on the process output of customer applications could lead to higher error rates to customers. Hence, instead of the entire transaction, individual critical fields within the application transaction were retained for a double level of checking. This reduced the overall daily time by 5280 min per day. A pilot improvement of this process change was monitored for 15 days, and the error rates were found within the tolerance limits and helped in obtaining the champion's consent for this implementation.
- *Increase in knowledge pool*: A cross-training schedule was created, and subject matter experts were used as trainers on all the products and processes handled in account opening and account maintenance. Classroom training for two hours per day for 10 days was conducted as per the schedule. Pre- and post-training

assessments were conducted, and scores were published to the project champion. At the end of the classroom sessions, the staff underwent on-the-job training in which they would complete a full transaction independently. This increased the knowledge-level across products from 50 to ~80%.

- *Reducing phone queries*: Account opening and maintenance application forms were standardized across locations, and critical information was made mandatory fields for customers to fill in the form. This reduced the number of calls bank branches needed to make for application-related queries. Daily management information system reports were published for pay instruction data, and an execution confirmation log was created for summary reports for branches to access data in real time. These changes saved ~500 min per day.
- *Redesigning cover sheet*: It was observed that, for a few bank branches there was a delay of ~48 h in obtaining cover sheets to process the transactions. The process of obtaining cover sheets was redesigned. Branches were instructed to enter the information on the cover sheet as part of the application submission, and separate cover sheets were eliminated. This reduced overall turnaround time, waiting time, and dependency on the cover sheet saving eight hours for the team.
- *Elimination of printing*: Printing of applications and relevant documents was eliminated. Alternatively, all bank documents were stored as pdf files on the bank's Intranet. This saved printing costs and time involved in printing and reduced the dependency on printers and associated maintenance costs. Total time saved due to the initiative was ~130 h per month.
- *Tactical automation*: An e-mail workflow system was designed using Microsoft (MS) Outlook mailbox rules by one of the bank's analysts. The algorithm created a group mailbox with different codes for each bank staff involved in processing. When the volumes of workflow into the group mailbox, the algorithm automatically sends a copy of the e-mail to the respective analyst in a defined sequence. This evenly divides the work into all analysts and enables effective resource-leveling. The algorithm also created a daily summary report to the respective managers for monitoring the productivity. This improvement led to a reduction of 40 h per day. The staff who contributed to this initiative was presented a special award by the bank management.

Control Phase: A control plan was proposed to the senior management to sustain the improvements. The process was monitored for one month using control charts. This data, collected on the employee utilization metric after improvements, was used to statistically validate the improvement using the 2-sample t-test, as it exhibited normality. Mean utilization after the improvement was optimized at 96.6%, with a standard deviation of 18.3%. The p value in the t-test at 95% confidence level confirmed that there was a significant change before and after the project. Further, the process capability test was performed and the process capability indexes Pp = 0.18 and Ppk = 0.12 were calculated, and the observed PPM value was found to be 636,363 defects and it was confirmed that the PIs contributed to reducing the PPM defects from 825,688 (Fig. 5.4). As a part of the project closure, an employee satisfaction survey was rolled out to check the level of

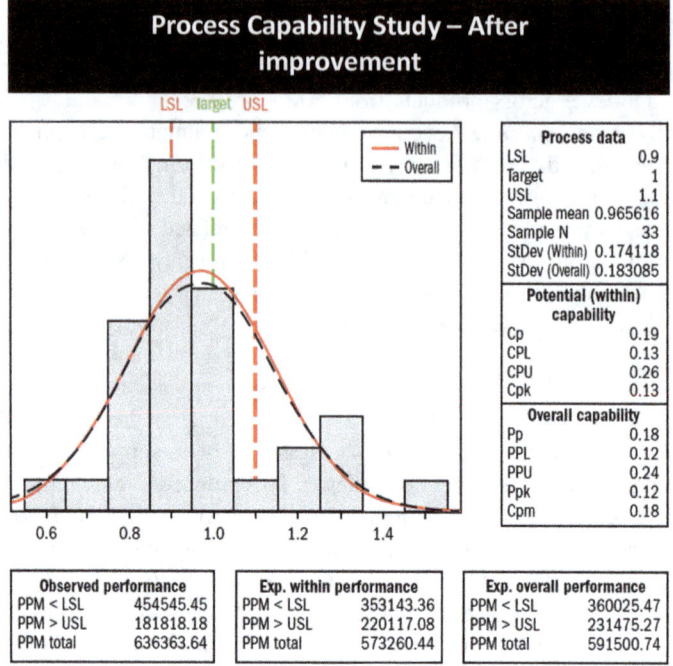

Fig. 5.4 Process capability post-improvements

employee morale post-improvement. A questionnaire was sent to all 90 staff, and 78 of them responded. Analysis of the responses revealed that 88% of the employees felt that the PIs were very helpful and changed their way of working. On the satisfaction level of staff, the mode value of the survey was nine out of ten. These results further confirmed that LSS not only optimized the employee utilization percentage, but also added to employee satisfaction.

5.4.2 Case B: Rejects Reduction in Accounts Opening of a Bank's Back Office

A large retail bank has its centralized back-office operations in India. The operations are responsible for processing the account opening forms which are submitted by the customers at different branches across the country. The output expected at the end of every transaction is a successfully opened customer account. The bank has three regional offices (at Bangalore, Delhi, and Mumbai) to facilitate the accumulation of the documents collected at different branches of the bank. The input documents come from the three regional offices to the back office on daily basis, for them to process the files and open the accounts. Account opening is a critical process for the bank because of increasing security and to avoid any fraud

5.4 Case Studies

by blacklisted people. At the same time, account opening process is a key process to bank from customer perspective; as account opening is the initial step or interaction which customer associates with the bank and hence plays a vital role to create an impression about the bank to the customer. Multi-level checks are performed by the regional offices and the central back office ensuring the completion and correctness of the application form and the required documentation (Sunder M2016).

Define: It was observed that approximately 10% of the account opening requests were rejected by the bank in last the one year. The bank's management team is concerned about this, realizing that they are missing 10 out of every 100 customers approaching them to have an association with the bank. Management after looking at the problem from a strategic perspective strongly felt that the root cause of the problem needs to be understood in order to find a robust fix. The improvement on the rejects percentage metric would impact the customer experience and also improves the customer base for the bank, alongside providing direct bottom-line benefits. A middle-level manager with LSS skill set at Black Belt level was approached by the management in order to take this business case as an opportunity for improvement, assigning as a project leader. The management team decided to reduce the account opening rejects percentage from the current ∼10–4.5% (striving toward 0%) in a time frame of six months, and thus, the target of the project has been arrived. The project followed LSS methodology in DMAIC approach for process improvement. A project charter was framed by the project leader which included a more precise background of the problem. The project charter was submitted to the bank's senior management team for their consensus to kick-start the project. A cross-functional project team was formed with assigned roles and responsibilities to execute the project as per the define phase of the DMAIC methodology. Detailed project charter is presented in Table 5.2.

Table 5.2 Project charter

Project charter	
Problem statement: Out of 28,497 accounts opening applications processed, 2720 (9.54%) of applications have been rejected by the bank for multiple reasons in the past 1 year. Stakeholders feel that the rejects percentage needs to be reduced for enhanced customer experience	**Goal statement**: To reduce the rejects percentage to below 4.5% from the current 9.54% striving toward zero, in a time frame of 6 months
Project scope: The project is scoped for the applications received from three regional offices located at Bangalore, Delhi, and Mumbai	**Project metric**: Rejects percentage = Number of Accounts opened/Number of accounts opening applications received
Project timeline: 6 months	**Project team**: Project leader: XXXXX (LSS Black Belt) Project champion: XXXXX Sponsor: XXXXX Other team members: XXX, XXX

The project team then looked at the process in great detail. Process mapping exercise was performed using swimlane method. Swimlane process map is preferred over other techniques, as it is considered as the best representation of the cross-functional processes. The name cross-functional means the whole work process crosses several functions (Robert 2011). Sequence of steps at bank branches, regional offices, and centralized back office are documented. The process was found to be fairly simple with four decision-making steps. There are multiple handoffs identified in the process through this exercise, which are further looked upon to identify opportunities for process simplification. Figure 5.5 shows the swimlane representation of the process map. The benefit of using the swimlane map is that the stakeholders who may not have complete knowledge of the process will be able to quickly identify the factors responsible for each activity through this way of depicting the process. This further serves as a visual supplement for written policies and procedures of the organization.

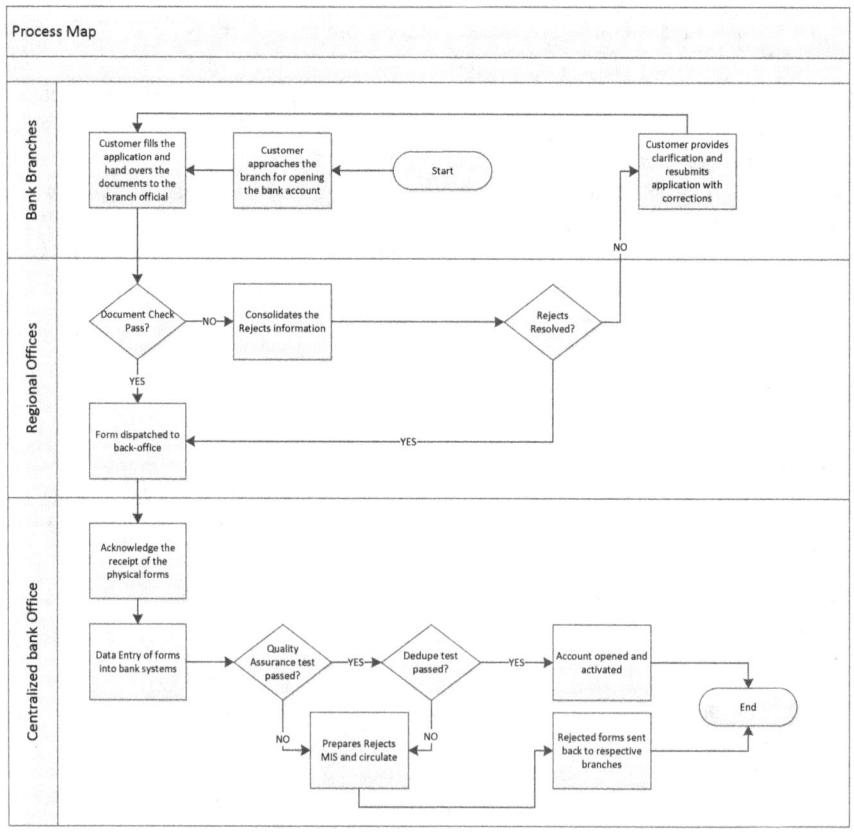

Fig. 5.5 Swimlane process map

5.4 Case Studies

Measure: Measurement system analysis (MSA) is then performed using Gauge R-R tool. This is performed as part of the measure phase to check whether the measurement system of the data is in-tact for further data collection and analysis or not. From the process mapping, it is very evident that the decision to open a customer bank account or not determines the rejects percentage of the bank. Hence, MSA is performed on the ability of the processors to correctly judge whether the customer application qualifies for opening the account or a reject. The repeatability, reproducibility, and accuracy of the measurement system are checked and found to be 80, 50, and 50%, respectively. The overall Gauge score (minimum value of repeatability, reproducibility, and accuracy) is inferred as 50%. Hence from Fig. 5.6, the current measurement system is not considered adequate to collect data and requires improvement.

In order to improve the measurement system, the following are implemented:

- Introduced a new training for regional office processors on policy change, strengthening the process of first level of quality checking activity. This is further proposed to be a recurring monthly activity.
- Implementation of standardized review and feedback format to the central back office.
- Promote usage of the exhaustive checklists at both regional and central offices for effective quality checking.
- Various changes implemented to the account opening form.
- Streamline and revamp the reject tracking process.

Waste analysis was then performed on the process. This helped the project manager to understand the process from the Lean perspective. Over-processing and transportation waste were identified to be predominant in the process. Multiple levels of inspection leading to over-processing were identified as opportunity for improvement. Moving the physical account opening forms from different locations to central back office was another prospect for process improvement.

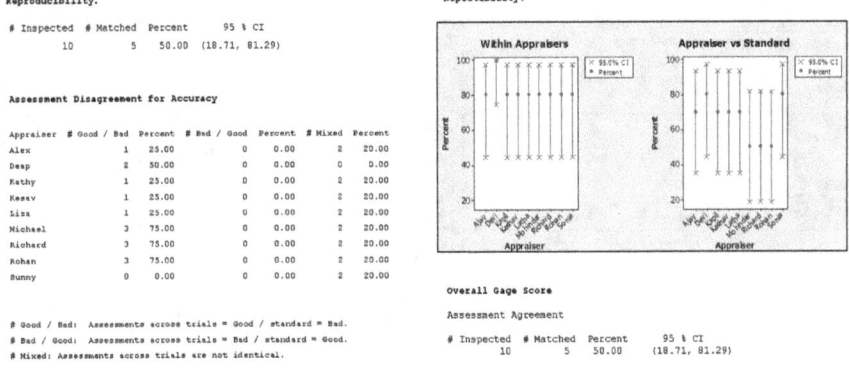

Fig. 5.6 Measurement system analysis

Post-implementing the improvements to the measurement system MSA is performed again. The repeatability, reproducibility, and accuracy score post-improvement were found to be 90, 80, and 90%, respectively. The overall gauge score is found to be 80%, and hence, it is concluded that the measurement system is now adequate enough and trustable to collect data. Data collection plan is then rolled out to the operations in order to collect data on the rejects percentage. Binomial process capability analysis was performed on the data with 95% confidence level. Binomial process capability technique is used here as the process outcome is binary (reject or no reject). The following observations are made from Fig. 5.7.

- The p-chart indicates that there are five points out of control above upper control limit. Points below lower control limit need not be worried upon as expectation is lower the better defectives. Overall process is found to be fairly stable.
- The chart of cumulative percentage defects shows that the estimate of the overall defective rate appears to be settling down around 7.07%.
- The rate of defectives does not appear to be much affected by the sample size.
- The process sigma (Z) is 1.47, and hence, the short-term sigma is 2.97 (i.e., 1.47 + 1.5 shift).
- The rejects percentage is reduced from 9.54 to 7.07% by improving the measurement system.

The process capability analysis further reinforced the need to improve the reject percentage metric for process improvement.

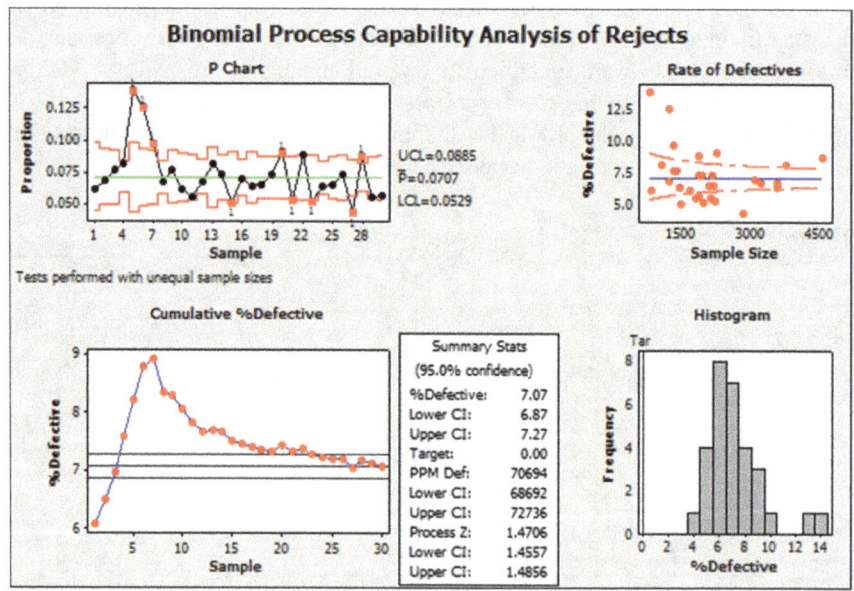

Fig. 5.7 Process capability (before project)

5.4 Case Studies

Analyze: The cross-functional stakeholders were then called upon for a brainstorming session, in order to understand the root causes of the problem. It is important to involve appropriate stakeholders at every stage of the LSS project, without which there could be bottlenecks in the project's success. It was observed that the participant groups were very hesitant to speak up about the process experience and observations in groups. Hence, the project manager chose to perform the brainstorming using the card method. The card method of brainstorming encourages participants to write the root cause as per their experience and observations and stick it over the whiteboard without mentioning their identity. This gave the candidates an opportunity to express themselves without panic or ambiguity. The ideas collected in the brainstorming session were then categorized using cause and effect diagram (Fig. 5.8) into four categories—sales, process, service providers, and policy. Across all four categories, eight potential causes of the problem were identified.

Pareto analysis was performed across different reasons leading to the higher reject percentage. The deep dive analysis on the data further revealed the percentage of rejects across the three regions—Bangalore, Mumbai, and Delhi. Hypothesis testing and other analysis techniques from LSS toolkit were applied on the causes identified in the brainstorming session. The below table summarizes the inferences arrived from the analysis phase of the project. All tests were performed with 95% confidence level (Table 5.3).

Alongside the usage of statistical and management tools of LSS summarized in Table 5.3, it is equally important to look at the process by on-floor observations.

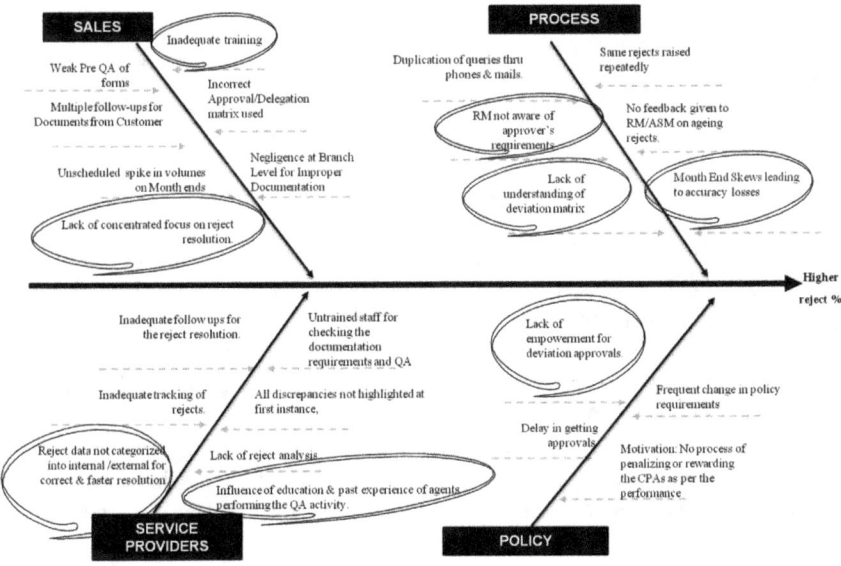

Fig. 5.8 Cause–effect diagram

Table 5.3 Causes of the problem

Test	Test statistics					Inference
Pareto analysis: To identify the vital-few reasons contributing to the higher rejects percentage	*Pareto Chart of REASONS*					Sign-related and name-related mismatch of data are the primary reasons contributing to 60% of the rejects
Correlation test: To check the impact of volumes processed on rejects percentage	Pearson correlation = 0.120 *P* value = 0.593					The *P* value is 0.59, which shows that there is no correlation between processed volumes and the rejects percentage
One-way ANOVA: To check the impact of calendar week on rejects percentage	Source	DF	SS	MS	F	P	The *P* value is 0.06, which is just above 0.05. Hence, it is concluded that there is no statistically significant impact of the week on rejects percentage
	Week	3	11.6	3.8	2.8	0.06	
	Level	N	Mean		St. Dev		
	Week 1	6	6.577		1.171		
	Week 2	6	6.924		1.145		
	Week 3	5	5.477		1.116		
	Week 4	5	7.571		1.240		
Multi-vari chart: To check the impact of education and past experience of the associates on rejects percentage	Multi-Vari Chart for Reject % by Education - Past Experience					• Reject percentage is high for undergraduates with less than 5 months experience in the process • Graduates irrespective of their past experience are performing good with less reject percentage • Among the <3 years exp agents, reject percentage by undergraduates is high

Not all problems are solved in board room; Gemba walks denote the action of going to see the actual process, understanding the work, and learning through asking questions. The benefits of Gemba walk include:

- On-floor observations provide the project managers with firsthand information about the process problems.
- Gemba walk provides associates with psychological benefits. By doing so, the manager is in a way conveying the associates that they are important for the progress of the organization and are playing a critical role in the process.

5.4 Case Studies

- Saves time of learning new process for a LSS consultant.
- Hidden waste in the process is not generally identified in brainstorming or data analysis. Gemba walks help the project managers to identify the waste in the process.
- Managers generally have an overview of the process. But it is the process associates who work on the process on day to day basis know the process in and out. Hence, asking the right questions to associates and learning through observations is essential in understanding the root causes of the problem.

Improve: Post-understanding the process through Gemba and analyzing the data using LSS toolkit, the project team is once again called for the brainstorming session. The theme of the brainstorming this time is to ideate for solutions in order to solve the problem. The project manager called in for 12 stakeholders from respective teams and explained them the causes of the problem and encouraged them to ideate for solutions to eradicate the root causes, to reduce the rejects percentage. Each improvement item is further extended with a control plan (shown in Table 5.4) in order to sustain the improvements. The management of the bank has provided support in order to implement the changes. Internal employees were used to accelerate change as per the improvement plan, without any substantial investment. Visual management dashboards are implemented as part of the project. The dashboards showcase the real status of the rejects on hourly basis displayed on the operations floor. This created awareness about the KPI performance against the target. This also improved the work culture of the associates. There was a mind-set change from manager-monitoring model to self-monitoring model. This is because the rejects percentage and other key metrics are displayed transparently to every floor against the names of the associates who rejected them. This created the responsibility toward the employees to express more accountability toward work, creating a significant behavioral change. Management team comprising of senior colleagues in the bank evaluated the project and found to be delightful.

Control: The project savings were documented as 1.6 million INR per year. The sigma value of the process is calculated post-improvements in order to validate the process capability (Fig. 5.9). Binominal process capability study is performed with the improved process. As shown in Fig. 5.9, the reject percentage has reduced to 3.4% post-improvement. The p-chart indicates that there is only 1 point out of control above UCL. Points below LCL need not be worried upon as expectation is lower the better defectives. The chart of cumulative percentage defects shows that the estimate of the overall defective rate appears to be settling down around 3.40%. The rate of defectives does not appear to be much affected by the sample size. The

Table 5.4 Improvement plan

Improvement	Control
Smart tips: An initiative to circulate one pager weekly knowledge sharing material over e-mail which explains the simple ways of working to generate effective output	A team leader is responsible for composing and circulating the e-mail
Checklist: A checklist is prepared for the associates to help them perform the decision making of accepting or rejecting the account at the central back office. Only few critical fields are mentioned as part of the checklist, eliminating the non-value-added activities	A physical checklist is pasted at every workstation in the central back office. The check sheets are reviewed and updated on quarterly basis by the team leaders
Signature mismatch: Signature matching software implemented at the branches, which helps in reducing the rejects relating to signature mismatch	Software maintenance team was made responsible to upgrade and to maintain the application
Name mismatch: Changes incorporated in the name mismatch policy to reduce the rejects	Policy review board to review the policy and make updating on a half-yearly basis
Electronic applications: The customer account opening forms at branches are replaced by online application forms with critical information as mandatory fields. The customer is further encouraged to initiate an electronic account opening process without coming to the branches	Net banking automated system is implemented to sustain the process
Training: Quarterly training analysis was made part of the back-office employee appraisal goals, and all associates are trained in all critical decision-making steps of the process	Training agenda was created which becomes part of the annual appraisal goals and evaluation of the employees
Elimination of cover letter: Process enhancements performed eliminating the cover letter. All applications and documents are scanned and sent electronically to the back office, without cover letter	Manual cover letter requirement eliminated, hence no control required

process Z is 1.82, and hence, the short-term sigma is 3.32 (i.e., 1.82 + 1.5 shift). Hence, the project successfully reduced the rejects percentage from ~10 to 3.4%. The project closure and success is communicated to all the stakeholders in the board meeting, and the project learning and the DMAIC approach were documented and circulated to the concerned parties via e-mail.

5.4 Case Studies

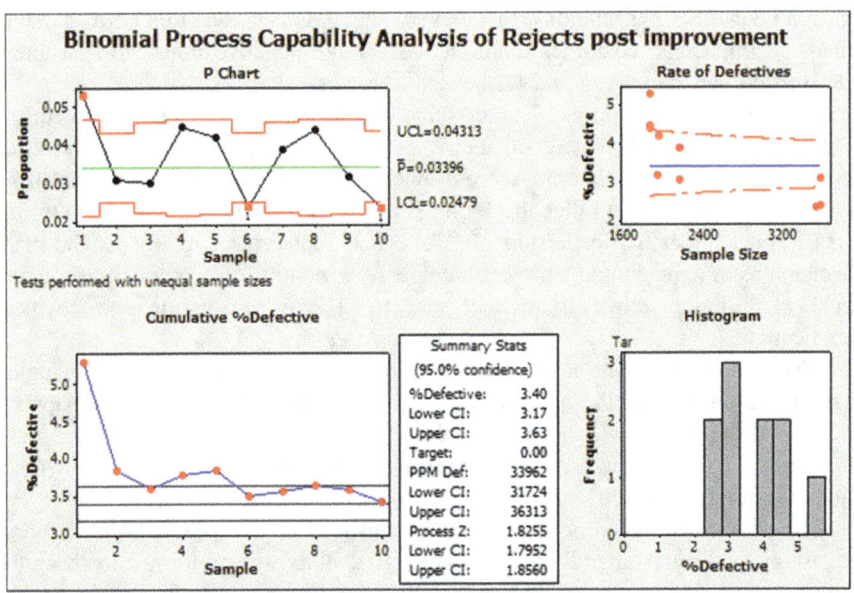

Fig. 5.9 Process capability (after project)

5.4.3 Case C: Accuracy Improvement in Payments Processing

The case study below describes how even a small proportion of defects become critical in a banking setting and how LSS can help in improving the process for customer satisfaction.

Define Phase: The initial interactions with the leadership team of the bank revealed that there have been frequent client escalations in the past with regard to the KPIs regarding client delivery. These include error rate, first pass yield, turn-around time, and accuracy. The Kano model questionnaire was adapted to prioritize the customer concerns. A questionnaire comprising 15 pairs of functional and dysfunctional questions was created and rolled out to 46 management teams. The functional–dysfunctional pairs of questions for every KPI were randomly shuffled. From the client groups, 32 representatives responded to the questionnaire reflecting a 69% response rate. The responses were analyzed with individual scores for each KPI and classified into "must-be needs," "one-dimensional needs," and "attractive needs."

This study based on frequencies of customer responses helped to identify the primary "must-be" concern for the clients as the accuracy KPI for the payments process. Hence, the project metric is chosen to be the defects per payment application. A deeper look at the past six months' baseline data revealed that on an average 13,000 payment applications per month were handled by a team of 10 FTE. Among these, 281 applications, with a defect rate of 2.16%, were found to be not meeting customer expectations. Since every single defect leads to a corresponding financial impact on customer funds, it has a huge negative impact on customer satisfaction and reputation and further led to rework.

A summary of the project charter submitted to the project champion, with the defined problem statement, goal, metric definition and the baseline performance details, is given in Table 5.5. A cross-functional team involving personnel from client base, bank's front office, back office, and information technology (IT) teams, was formed under the leadership of LSS Black Belt project manager. The management team agreed upon a project timeline of 6 months to accomplish the project goal of bringing down the defect rate to <1% in processing the payment applications.

Measure Phase: The LSS project manager performed a process mapping exercise to understand the payment processing process in detail. Process maps are models of the workflow, and the swimlane process map is considered to be most appropriate to understand a process with multiple handoffs across different functions of the organization.

The data measurement system was tested using Gauge repeatability and reproducibility analysis (Gauge R-R). The Gauge R-R study was performed to check the accuracy and precision of the measurement system to correctly judge whether the defects are real defects or only apparent defects due to variation in the gauge. This study revealed that repeatability, reproducibility, and accuracy of the measurement system were 85, 80, and 90%, respectively. The overall Gauge score (minimum value of repeatability, reproducibility, and accuracy) was inferred to be 80%. Hence, the current measurement was considered adequate.

A data collection plan was devised by including a random sample of 3200 records of data. The collected data was tested for determining the process capability and the sigma level using the DPMO criterion since the project metric involved a discrete data-type (Sunder M and Antony 2015). Out of the 3200 records of applications, 69 did not meet the customer expectations and were considered as defects (Table 5.6). The corresponding DPMO value was 21,563, with yield at 97.84% and the process sigma value at 3.52.

Analyze Phase: A brainstorming session was conducted with the cross-functional team involving senior management personnel including the project

Table 5.5 Summary of the project charter

Project KPI	Metric selection			Metric performance		Project goal	Project duration
	Defect definition	Project metric	Metric type	Baseline period	Baseline value		
Accuracy of payment application	Any payment transaction not meeting the customer requirements	Defects %	Discrete	6 months	Defect % = 2.16%	Defect % < 1%	6 months

5.4 Case Studies

Table 5.6 Process capability with baseline data

Defects	Units	Total opportunities	Defects per unit	Defects per million opportunities	Process yield	Sigma value
69	3200	3200	0.0216	21,563	97.84%	3.52

champion. This enabled understanding the reasons for the defects in payment processing. The causes voiced by the group were grouped under five categories, viz. material, machine, method, case resolution, and people. The causes identified were validated (Table 5.7) using hypothesis testing.

A Pareto chart is commonly used to prioritize where action and process changes should be focused upon through identifying the vital-few causes leading to a majority of the problems. Here, it was used to:

1. identify top contributors (analysts) of errors in payments processing,
2. identify the key process steps where frequent defects occurred, and
3. identify the vital-few reasons for errors in processing applications.

The 5-Why analysis technique was used (Fig. 5.10) to identify the root causes. Toyota prescribed simple tools whenever possible and placed great emphasis on root cause analysis identifying robust solutions using the 5-Why analysis. The

Table 5.7 Pareto analysis

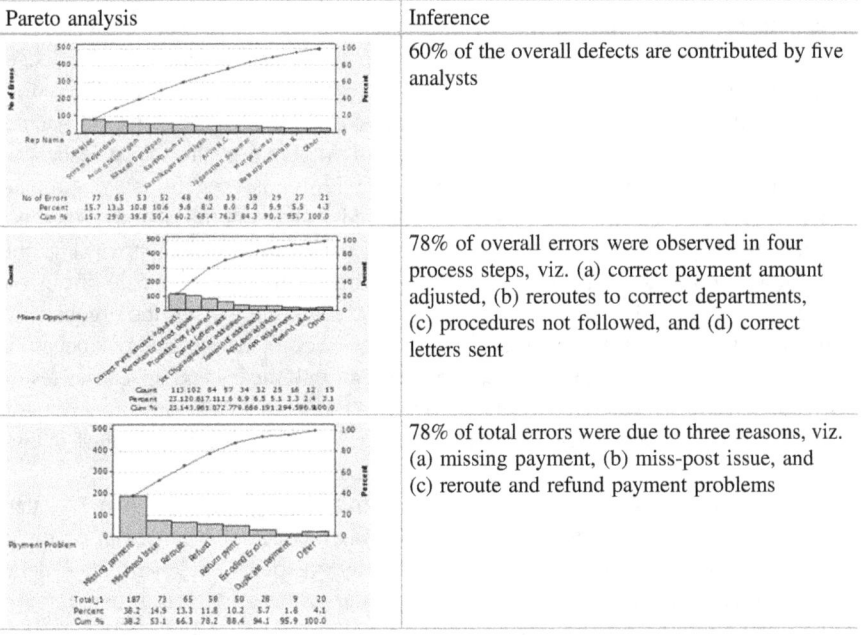

Pareto analysis	Inference
	60% of the overall defects are contributed by five analysts
	78% of overall errors were observed in four process steps, viz. (a) correct payment amount adjusted, (b) reroutes to correct departments, (c) procedures not followed, and (d) correct letters sent
	78% of total errors were due to three reasons, viz. (a) missing payment, (b) miss-post issue, and (c) reroute and refund payment problems

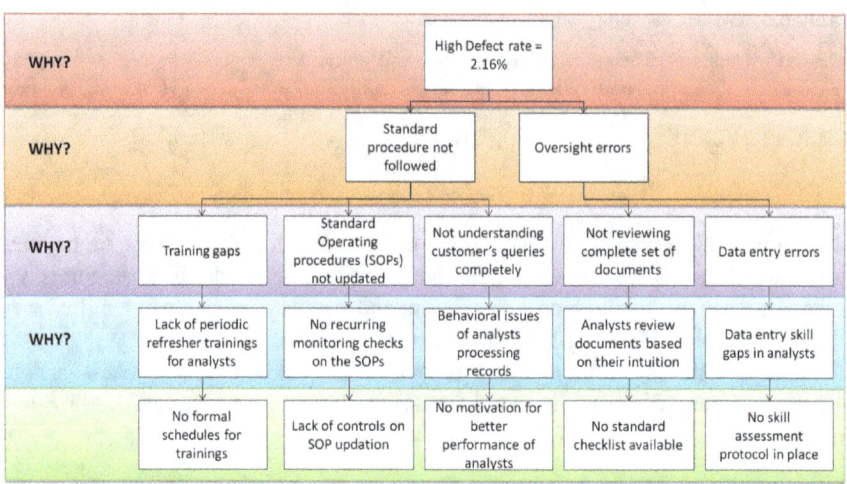

Fig. 5.10 5-Why analysis

5-Why technique is not a statistical method but is common in practice in LSS projects. Although the traditional 5-Why technique requires that the "why" question be asked five times, in this analysis the why the question was asked only four times. The asking of the "why" could be stopped if common sense reveals that no more "why" questions are needed to solve the problem.

Improve Phase: Another brainstorming session was conducted with the relevant stakeholders for the purpose of identifying solutions. The project manager was involved in an industry benchmarking in parallel to identify industry good practices for implementation. An improvement plan was devised and presented to the project champion and the sponsor for obtaining their consent and sponsorship for implementation. Upon understanding the proposed improvements, the senior leadership team directed the project manager to come up with a cost–benefit analysis for the proposal. A cost–benefit analysis was prepared based on the stated preference method. In the context of project management using industry benchmarking, this method was found advantageous. According to this method, solutions are prioritized based on the personal valuations of an activity by assessing the cost the organization is prepared to accept or pay for a specific new service or an incremental risk benefit in an existing service. After a few follow-up meetings with the leadership team, a few of the proposed improvements were approved. An overview of the improvements signed off for implementation involving a total cost of $26,500 is presented below.

- *Payment letter simplification*: It was found that there were more than 12 letters which the bank sent to its customers pertaining to various instances of customer service, which included missing payment letter, misplaced payment letter, delay in payment letter, and refund letter. These letters were sent to customers through e-mail using MS Outlook. As a part of the improvement, MS Outlook templates

were created, which, by using a predefined algorithm, could automatically generate and send letters in pdf format to customers. Further, the body of the letter was simplified to meet the customer specifications. This reduced the processing errors at the letter generation stage leading to saving rework time by 1600 h per year.
- *Interest charge calculation*: Difficulties faced by analysts in issuing appropriate interest charge to customers, due to complex methods were simplified by refining the procedure. An MS Excel-based interest calculator was developed by the project team using Visual Basic. The interest calculator reduced the number of defects and the cycle time by 270 h per annum.
- *Process manual standardization*: The lack of standardized procedures resulted in a huge variation in the processing of payment applications by analysts. High-impact errors in process steps were identified and elaborate steps, and procedures were drafted. Unclear and incomplete procedures were eliminated. A comprehensive client procedure manual was created online to enable a search feature for helping analysts to search for the required information and to refer and process the applications correctly.
- *Process knowledge and cross-training*: Lack of process knowledge due to training gaps presented another key reason for poor performance. As a part of the annual training budget, quarterly classroom-based, instructor-led refresher trainings were imparted to the analysts. The payment gateway changes and compliance trainings were incorporated as a part of the new-joiner induction process. The trained staff was job-shadowed by a process mentor selected from a pool of subject matter experts of the bank. The training outcomes were linked to the analysts' performance and monitored closely by the team leads and reported through a monthly dashboard to senior management.
- *Internal award system*: In order to improve morale and create a competitive environment for error-free delivery, an internal monthly award scheme was introduced. Cash prizes were awarded to the analysts who performed consistently across a month with zero defects in the payments processing.
- *Checklist creation*: From the Pareto analysis, it was evident that frequently occurring defects were observed from four key process steps. A checklist of all the key review steps, documents, and approvals was created. A pamphlet of the same was placed at the analysts' processing desks.
- *Workflow automation*: The existing workflow system was calibrated with the smart analytics feature to generate real-time reports highlighting the defect levels. A Pugh matrix was used to identify the workflow options available in the market. The automation of the workflow tool was achieved with the help of the bank's IT team. User acceptance testing was performed for 2 weeks across different business scenarios and the enhanced workflow went live. This enabled the team to reduce and monitor the defects and saved ~ 1000 h per year.

Due to the dependency on other functional teams and delays in obtaining approval from sponsors for implementing the improvements, the project was estimated to miss the original schedule of 6 months. This was highlighted to the senior management as a project risk and approvals obtained on the revised timeline with an extension of another 2 months. This increased the project resource cost by $8000.

Control Phase: The control phase of the project involved two important deployments: (a) Control tracker to sustain the improvements and (b) control chart to monitor the project metric performance. With the extended timelines, the improvements were monitored for 2 months. A control tracker was created for each of the improvements implemented. The IT team agreed to take the responsibility of the workflow tool deployed as a part of the project. Supervisory controls were deployed for the internal awards, checklists, and cross-training. There was no separate control required, since the payment tool simplification was a mistake-proofing improvement using templates. The managers agreed to verify and revise the interest charge calculator on a half-yearly basis. After the improvements, daily defects data was collected for 2 months and plotted on the control chart for monitoring the defect rate. Of a total of 24,055 applications processed in the two months, 224 defects were found reflecting a defect rate of 0.9%. Table 5.8 shows the reduction in the defect rate from 2.16% (before project) to 0.9% (after project). A U-chart (Fig. 5.11) is used to display this as the project metric is discrete data of defects with unequal sample sizes of payment applications. Process capability was checked at the end of the project. It was found that the LSS project reduced the

Table 5.8 Process capability post-improvement

Defects	Units	Total opportunities	Defects per unit	DPMO	Process yield	Sigma value
224	24,055	24,055	0.0093	9312	99.07%	3.85

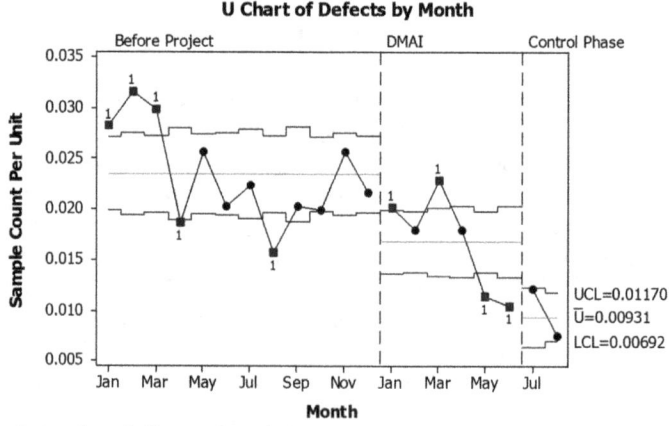

Fig. 5.11 Defect rate—before versus after LSS project

DPMO value from 21,563 (before the project) to 9312 (after the project) with an improved process yield of 99.07% and a sigma value of 3.85. Overall bottom-line impact of the project was found to be a recurring saving of ~$560,000 per annum. Alongside the tangible benefits, all the staff members of the bank who participated in this LSS project conveyed their positive feedback on the experiential learning they underwent. The project also received a special appreciation from the bank's leadership team.

5.5 Lessons Learned and Managerial Implications

The above case studies provide evidence of the successful application of LSS in BFS, specifically in the banking domain and the associated multiple benefits. Since the probability of occurrence of defects is higher, and the corresponding tolerance and business impact consequences are critical in consumer banks, the necessity for application of LSS projects deserves emphasis. LSS, with a focus on (a) reducing defects, (b) process variations and waste, and (c) striving to improve "value" with customer centricity, is relevant for the BFS context. Since the BFS setting operates at a risk of losing customer satisfaction for any process changes, a systematic approach to problem solving such as LSS is highly essential for Banks. The business outcomes observed from the above case studies include both tangible and intangible benefits. The tangible benefits include KPI improvement, cost savings, and increased process efficiencies. Intangible benefits include employee satisfaction and morale, CI culture building, and enabler for staff learning and empowerment.

5.5.1 LSS as a Systems Approach for Process Improvement

According to systems thinking theories, a whole system failure may coexist alongside functional success. In the context of this study, the success of one LSS project need not directly mean the success of LSS deployment in a bank. From the above case studies, it is evident that an LSS project need not necessarily improve the entire organization or processes. The sigma value or process capability (DPMO or PPM) which is presented in the above cases is merely an indication of a KPI chosen for the improvement but does not indicate the overall process itself. For example, in Case C, by successfully completing an LSS project on the payments processing process, it cannot be concluded that the entire payment processing system has improved. Though the project definitely improved "accuracy," there could be other KPIs like "turnaround time of processing a payment" that may (or may not) have any impact due to this project. Hence, LSS projects should focus on a primary KPI improvement while concurrently monitoring other relevant KPIs. Project managers should be mindful of secondary KPIs that may have a positive impact or negative impact on the improvements through the LSS projects. Hence, LSS project managers should break the narrow project-only approach and see operational processes from a systems perspective for effecting process improvements. Over a period of time, many such successful LSS projects in the same setting will lead to LSS deployment impacting the cultural elements and bottom-line benefits. This needs to be tested further as an extension of this study.

5.5.2 Identification of Correct LSS Candidates

Since banks are prone to high risk due to their dealing with customer's funds, it is essential that right project selection criteria are adapted for the LSS projects. Capturing the VOC would be the first step where LSS recommends tools like interviews, customer dashboard analysis, questionnaires, customer satisfaction score analysis, and balanced scorecard analysis. Then LSS tools like Kano model help in prioritizing the VOC and further tools like CTQ tree for identifying the right KPIs aligned with the VOC. As a part of the LSS deployment, it is important to use intuition to discriminate LSS candidates from overall project opportunities. Assignments where solutions are known a priori do not require structured problem-solving approaches, and proper governance should suffice. These are "quick-kills" when the desired business impact is low, as the time and effort to implement known solutions is usually minimal. Lean would suffice for project candidates where the estimated business impact is high for a known solution. Business cases involving high impact and without a priori clues about root causes of problems or solutions are best fits for LSS projects. Table 5.9 represents a suggested matrix for banks embarking upon the LSS journey for the right selection of project candidates. LSS projects focus on root causes of problems for identifying robust and long-lasting solutions, while "quick-kills" would only offer temporary solutions.

5.5.3 LSS Project Management Is a Subset of LSS Deployment

From the above two cases, it is apparent that though LSS projects delivered cost savings to the respective functional units of the two consumer banks under study, it is not astute to comment on the bottom-line impact creation. The key learning here is that LSS project management and LSS deployment in the organizations are to be considered as two different efforts. In fact, LSS project management is merely a subset of LSS deployment. A culture of CI in a bank cannot be created by

Table 5.9 Project selection criteria

Business impact	A priori solutions	
	Unknown	Known (less time/effort)
High	First priority LSS projects	Lean projects
Low	Second priority LSS projects	Quick-kills

5.5 Lessons Learned and Managerial Implications

conducting one or two LSS projects. Despite the benefits observed from the above case studies, the bottom-line impact can be created only by conducting many such LSS projects for sustaining a CI culture. For example, in Case B, the bank improved its payment processing accuracy from 97.84 to 99.07% through one LSS project. A subsequent endeavor aiming to improve accuracy further from 99.07 to 99.99% could be a follow-up LSS project.

5.5.4 Management of Stakeholders in LSS Projects

LSS project management demands focused management of stakeholders. In the above cases, right from the project identification to monitoring and control, this aspect has been an important criterion for success. It is evident from the above cases that LSS projects involve a wide variety of stakeholders across different levels of the organization within and across functions. Though the outcomes of the changes have led to benefits, the process of change has been challenging. In Case B, though logical conclusions were arrived after rigorous data analysis and benchmarking, the improvement plan presented to the management of the bank was not endorsed. Only after multiple follow-up meetings, the change recommendation plan was partly approved for implementation. Hence, involving, informing, and influencing the right stakeholders at appropriate phases of the DMAIC project are a critical success factor in LSS project management. Previous research shows that top-management commitment is a critical success factor for LSS projects. But it is observed that although top management is an important element of the total stakeholder community, project success also depends on other stakeholders. We conclude that total stakeholders' participation and commitment are essential for LSS projects. The term "stakeholder" needs to be understood with a broader mind-set and includes customers, frontline staff, managers, process owners, and top management.

5.5.5 Change Leadership for LSS Projects

In any change management initiative, resistance to change is inevitable and LSS is not an exception. This makes leadership become critical. While change must be well managed, it also requires effective leadership to be introduced and sustained. The key reasons for resistance generally include parochial self-interest, misunderstanding of change, low-tolerance to change, and different assessments of the situation. Alongside these, in the context of consumer banks, the other contributors include the high risk and high impact of the nature of the banking processes. Every LSS project leads to process changes. In the banking case studies presented, it has led to people and cultural changes as well. For example, in Case A, the project not only improved the employee utilization rate, but also improved the satisfaction and morale of the bank staff, while effecting cost efficiencies. Hence, education and communication, participation and involvement, facilitation and support, negotiation and agreement are important attributes which are recommended for LSS project managers to smoothen the progress of LSS implementation. Relevant usage of LSS tools like failure mode and effects analysis (FMEA), probabilistic risk assessment (PRA), risk assessment dashboards could be handy in LSS projects. Appropriate understanding of LSS as a management strategy, and not merely as a toolkit, is essential for leadership vision to enable the usage of LSS for realizing the bank's mission. Hence, organizational leaders need to realize that LSS is not merely a project manager's job but is very much a part of the leadership agenda for success. A successful deployment of LSS requires leadership and business processes, and these two inputs are not mutually exclusive.

5.6 Summary of This Chapter

LSS has made a significant impact on how service organizations handle process-related problems. As a CI practice, LSS becomes more helpful in BFS firms as every defect could have a significant financial impact leading to customer dissatisfaction, damaging the overall reputation of a bank. LSS also enables building and retaining customer relationships for banks by delivering defect-free services. The banking industry with operations such as transaction-based back offices, call centers, equity research, and transcription services has the obligation to maintain the service levels by improving and maintaining the KPIs at an optimum level, which is essential for the banks to create positive impressions and a strong brand. The three case studies presented in this chapter are classic examples of how LSS can transform BFS processes and the mind-set of frontline employees and the management.

Alongside presenting the operational benefits via the application of LSS in banking, this chapter serves as a strong foundation for future research in this area. However, the extent of applicability of LSS in BFS depends on the interest, rigor, and scope of the banking operations. It is further concluded that LSS project management is merely a subset of LSS deployment in banks. Both tangible and intangible benefits of LSS are evident in the consumer banking context from the above two real-world case evidences. Further, research is needed to strengthen the understanding of LSS from the process, human, and culture perspectives in BFS organizations.

References

Dan, S. (2004). *How six sigma transformed HSBC's US futures business*. Available at www.jmp.com/software/success/pdf/hsbc_sixsigma.pdf. Accessed September 2, 2014.

Delgado, C., Ferreira, M., & Castelo Branco, M. (2010). The implementation of lean Six Sigma in financial services organizations. *Journal of Manufacturing Technology Management, 21*(4), 512–523.

De Koning, H., Does, R. J., & Bisgaard, S. (2008). Lean Six Sigma in financial services. *International Journal of Six Sigma and Competitive Advantage, 4*(1), 1–17.

References

Eisenhardt, K. (1989). Building theories from case study research. *Academy of Management Review, 14*(2), 532–550.

George, M. L. (2002). *Lean six sigma: Combining six sigma quality with lean speed/Michael L George*. USA: McGraw-Hill.

Hoffman, T. (2006). *Bank of America: Investing in Six Sigma*. Available at www.computerworld.com/s/article/265873/Investing_in_Six_Sigma?taxonomyId¼14&pageNumber¼3. Accessed September 1, 2014.

Lokkerbol, J., Does, R., de Mast, J., & Schoonhoven, M. (2012). Improving processes in financial service organizations: where to begin? *International Journal of Quality and Reliability Management, 29*(9), 981–999.

Online Source. (2012). *Lean six sigma success stories in financial services*. Available at www.goleansixsigma.com/lean-six-sigma-success-stories-inthe-financial-services-industry/. Accessed July 12, 2017.

Peteros, R. G., & Maleyeff, J. (2015). Using Lean Six Sigma to improve investment behavior. *International journal of Lean Six Sigma*.

Robert, D. (2011). *The basics of process mapping* (2nd ed.). Taylor & Francis Group.

Sunder M, V. (2016). Rejects reduction in a retail bank using Lean Six Sigma. *Production Planning and Control, 27*(14), 1131–1142.

Sunder M, V., & Antony, J. (2015). Six-sigma for improving top-box customer satisfaction score for a banking call centre. *Production Planning & Control, 26*, 1291–1305.

Sunder M, V., Ganesh, L. S., Marathe, R. R. (2019). Lean Six Sigma in consumer banking—An empirical inquiry. *International Journal of Quality and Reliability Management*, https://doi.org/10.1108/ijqrm-01-2019-0012.

Wang, F. K., & Chen, K. S. (2010). Applying Lean Six Sigma and TRIZ methodology in banking services. *Total Quality Management, 21*(3), 301–315.

Woods, R. (2010a). *Australian bank to revamp IT with Lean Six Sigma*. Available at www.isixsigma.com/industries/financial-services/australian-bank-revamp-it-lean-six-sigma. Accessed September 2014.

Woods, R. (2010b). *Scorecards help South African bank reap savings*. Available at www.isixsigma.com/consultants/balanced-scorecard-consultants/scorecards-help-south-africanbank-reapsavings. Accessed September 2014.

Yin, R. K. (2003). *Case study research: Design and methods* (3rd ed.). Thousand Oaks, CA: Sage.

6. Lean Six Sigma as a Dynamic Capability in Banking Firms

An overview of literature reveals the application of LSS through case studies, action research, and frameworks across different industry sectors. LSS has not attracted the same level of conversation about theory development and implications for competitive advantage as TQM (Douglas and Judge 2001; Su et al. 2014). Previous studies by Dobrzykowski et al. (2016) and Anand et al. (2009) studied Lean from a dynamic capabilities lens, but the nature of LSS as a dynamic capability (DC) has not been examined in the literature. This Chapter aims to explore the strategic value of LSS through iterative triangulation using existing literature and case data. It offers an evolutionary dynamic perspective of LSS through inductive research which helps generate valuable propositions for theory building. Comparative analysis of cases using the corresponding data brings together literature streams that have been previously disconnected. A triangulation of literature review understandings with cross-case analysis is used. These are refined for theory building towards strategic applications of LSS. For understanding these strategic orientations of LSS, it is important to understand what organizational capabilities are. In general, an organizational capability is a firm's ability to manage resources, (such as employees, finances, infrastructure, processes and systems) effectively to gain an advantage over competitors. The company's organizational capabilities must focus on the business's ability to meet customer demand.

6.1 Organizational Capabilities

Capabilities enable superior performance because they help solve complex problems. Strategic management thinkers have depicted organizational capabilities in different ways. A few authors addressed "capabilities" as a colloquial expression (Collis 1994; Schreyögg and Kliesch-Eberl 2007), while a few others termed them as "core competence" (Prahalad and Hamel 1990; Bonjour and Micaelli 2010). A leading text of the 1960s (Learned 1969) noted that "the capability of an organization is its demonstrated and potential ability to accomplish against the opposition of circumstance or competition, whatever it sets out to do." In other words, capabilities represent a reliable pattern of cognitive problem-solving architecture composed of complex inter-linked sets of actions in firms, which are practical and bound to performance (Helfat and Peteraf 2003). Despite the emphasis of the resource-based view (RBV), which claims "resources" as the fundamental building blocks of competitive advantage in firms (Barney 1991), theorists viewed capabilities as a key dimension of a firm's heterogeneity (Nelson and Winter 1973) that enables idiosyncrasy or inimitability towards creating competitive advantage. Amit and Schoemaker (1993) argued that "capabilities" are different from resources, and it is capabilities that form the basis of competitive advantage in firms. They defined capabilities as "a firm's capacity to deploy its resources, usually in combination, using organizational processes, to affect a desired end." Unlike resources, capabilities are based on developing, carrying, and exchanging information through the firm's intellectual capital. Even earlier, several authors used different labels while referring to capabilities. For example, Itami (1981) referred to these as information-based "invisible assets." Similarly, a few others called them as "non-tradable assets" that are (a) developed by and belong to the human capital, (b) accumulated within the firm, (c) tacit, and (d) born of organizational learning through path dependency.

Grant (1991) positioned capabilities above resources in his strategy analysis framework, where he mentioned that resources are the source of a firm's capabilities, and further, capabilities are the source of competitive advantage. Teece et al. (1997) claimed that the term "capabilities" emphasizes the key role of strategic management in appropriately adapting, integrating, and reconfiguring internal and external organizational skills, resources, and functional competences to match the requirements of a changing environment. A few authors explained organizational capabilities as being fundamental to firms' abilities to solve their organizational problems effectively. Winter (2003) defined capabilities as high-level routines that enable repeated and reliable performance of activities, in contrast to ad hoc activities that do not reflect practiced or patterned behavior. Helfat et al. (2007) stated that the term "capability" implies an organizational capacity to perform a particular activity in a reliable or at least minimally satisfactory manner. Capabilities change or evolve over time (Teece 2014), and hence, experience accumulation and path dependency become important (Protogerou et al. 2011). More recent work, however, suggests that mere experience accumulation does not suffice for capability development and sustenance. Codifying the experiences for organizational learning becomes critical, where these routines manifest in the array of organizational practices towards creating competitive advantage in firms (Heimeriks et al. 2012). Though several scholars often consider capabilities theories as an extension to RBV, capabilities address intended modifications of the resource-bases for creation of knowledge-bases towards organizational learning (Zollo and Winter 2002). Hence, in the context of deriving strategic value in organizations, resources become meaningless in the absence of capabilities which account for the purposeful modifications of the resource base (Schilke et al. 2018).

6.1 Organizational Capabilities

Several authors represented various typologies of capabilities (Hine et al. 2013). Collis (1994) expressed capabilities in four categories, viz., a firm's resources which reflect an ability to perform the basic functional activities, dynamic improvements to the activities of the firm, intrinsic value creators to develop novel strategies ahead of competitors, and meta-capabilities which are related to the learning-to-learn ability to outperform the competitors. Danneels (2002) proposed a similar structure for capabilities—the first-order capabilities which enable achievement of individual tasks and the second-order capabilities which enable firms to create or renew the first order capabilities. Winter (2003) represented capabilities as zero-, first- and higher-order capabilities in his capability hierarchy. He described ordinary capabilities (zero- and first-order) as those which involve administrative, operational and technical purposes that are essential to accomplish day-to-day tasks through which a firm makes its living. These are also called as operational capabilities (OCs) as they enable the firm to execute its main operating activities such as making and selling products or delivering services (Zahra et al. 2006).

According to Teece et al. (1997), resources of the firm constitute firm-specific capabilities which cannot create competitive advantage as they are internal to the firm, while consciously created higher-order capabilities, with unique attributes to build, integrate, or reconfigure the firm-specific capabilities while interacting with the environment, are termed as "dynamic capabilities" (DCs). These can create sustained competitive advantage in firms (Teece et al. 1997). Similarly, Eisenhardt and Martin (2000) defined DCs as organizational and strategic processes that could modify or integrate the resource-bases. Zollo and Winter (2002) and Helfat (2007) both classified capabilities in two levels, viz. operating routines/OCs and DCs. Later, Ambrosini and Bowman (2009) further classified DCs into incremental DCs, renewable DCs, and regenerative DCs. We can observe that though there existed differences in labelling the classification elements, scholars broadly categorized capabilities into ordinary capabilities (OCs) and dynamic capabilities (DCs), with one or more further levels/orders in each of these categories.

6.2 Dynamic Capabilities

The founding thinkers (Teece et al. 1997) defined the DCs approach as a firm's ability to alter its resource configurations by applying certain capabilities for adapting to changing environments and to achieve new forms of competitive advantage. The term "Dynamic" refers to the capacity to renew existing competencies for gaining flexibility while dealing with a changing environment. The term "Capabilities" emphasizes the key role of strategic management in appropriately adapting, integrating, and reconfiguring internal and external organizational resources and competencies to match the requirements of changing environments or even influence them in desired ways. Teece and Pisano (2003) suggested that a firm's DCs are determined by: (i) processes—managerial and organizational "routines," (ii) positions—current endowments of technology, customer bases, and suppliers, and (iii) paths—available strategic alternatives. The term "capability," in the strategic context of a firm, should serve two fundamental purposes, viz., performance and coordination of activities (Helfat and Peteraf 2003).

DCs work differently than OCs, which are generally static and operate independently (Sunder M et al. 2019a). Hence, DCs cannot be easily replicated, integrated, or imitated by competitors. They cannot be transferred, in a complete sense, between different firms because of the attendant interdependencies in the firms' resources, routines, and systems, all of which make it impossible to change one without another. Enterprises with stronger DCs are more flexible and adaptive to changing environments and hence more successful too (Teece 2014). Thus, DCs provide a foundation for sustaining competitive difference over time (Teece 2007). However, the magnitude of a DC varies from firm to firm for the same functionality. For example, in the e-commerce industry, firms like Amazon, E-bay, and Alibaba.com have effective online-sales service capability but at different levels of functionality. Further, the characterization of a DC is based on the context of the firm. For example, for a firm which produces and sells products, R&D capability is a DC for new product development but an operational capability for an independent R&D lab (Winter 2003).

Teece and Pisano (1994) highlighted the example of the Lean production system as a DC in Fujimoto Inc. By deploying Lean, they adapted distinctive shop-floor practices and processes cutting across skilled resources, principles, and systems of the firm contributing a culture of continuous improvement. It could be argued that Lean has been adopted by many other firms today, but every firm's Lean practice is unique and based on its interlock with its routines and resources. Another example could be Canon which uses its expertise in optics to serve markets as diverse as cameras, copiers, and semi-conductor equipment. Canon's competitive advantage is thus a result of its policy management across markets, which is not easily seen or understood by its rivals (Witcher et al. 2008). Canon does use collaborative forms of cross-functional management, through Hoshin Kanri (Policy Management) which served them as a DC to meet this purpose. Another example, implied through the case of Coca-Cola in India which has enjoyed great success due to their product branding DCs, concerns the challenge they faced due to the rapidly reducing groundwater. The government began shutting down Coca-Cola plants in India in 2010. Learning from the demand and the dynamics of the environment, the company devised ways of saving water including rain water harvesting and started branding themselves as a socially responsible organization, which further increased their success in the Indian market.

6.3 Approach to Study the Strategic Orientations

Since the strategic contributions of LSS for enabling competitive advantage in firms have not been sufficiently researched upon, the inductive research described here helps generate valuable propositions for theory building. Qualitative data obtained from three global banking firms over a period of three years has been used. The data collection exercise involved multiple rounds of interviews with select top- and mid-management personnel, site visits, participation in LSS project meetings and execution, study of management archives, and reported data on public domains. For triangulation, the data was synthesized with the results noted from the research literature on both LSS and DCs, which were studied independently by previous researchers. A cross-comparison of the case studies is then performed.

Purposive sampling, a non-probability sampling method was used to select cases that span different contextual settings. This contributes to increased generalizability. First, several global banks that claimed to have recently started LSS deployment practices were approached. Secondly, only those banks that attempted any CI practice before embarking upon their LSS journey were considered. Then, the selection was scoped to those banks that served customers across multiple banking streams (like consumer banking, commercial banking, investment banking, wealth management, etc.). This filter was added to incorporate the diversity in the banks' processes. Among several such banking firms, three multinational banks (hereafter called AA, BB, and CC) agreed to participate.

The purposive sampling helped in identifying banks with varying diversity in their tenure, geographical and business spread, number of employees, stability of operations, and financial performance. Among the three participant banks, "AA" claimed that they had a positive experience of Lean deployment for about two years before embarking upon their LSS journey. "BB" commenced their LSS deployment without any maiden Lean or Six Sigma experience; however, they declared that their staff were engaged in CI initiatives in their own interest. Bank "CC" declared that they practiced Lean and Six Sigma as two different CI programs before officially rolling-out their LSS program.

The first set of interviews was conducted with the top-management executives and their managers. During the interviews, the informants were probed with open-ended, cascading questions[1] related to the LSS deployment practices and their relevant features, viz., the motivational drivers for the banks' LSS journey, input factors that the banks considered as key ingredients of their LSS programs, and influencing factors including both endogenous and exogenous factors. The respondents were encouraged to discuss these aspects in as much detail as they

---

[1] The term "cascading questions" is used to denote questions that logically build upon responses to prior questions that arise from the response to an opening question. The total set of questions for any specific respondent need not necessarily be identical to that for other respondents. However, the entire set of questions posed to all respondents, as well as the entire set of corresponding responses serve as a basis to examine the subject, viz., LSS deployment practices and relevant features, as an integrated whole. Here, the researchers are responsible for the act of conceptual integration of the various components of the subject and providing the necessary justifications.

could. These interactions also helped in understanding how their LSS programs were aligned with their overall bank's strategy and priorities. Performance data over a three-year period, obtained from the respective organizational archival sources, helped further verify these patterns. These served as a starting point in deep-diving into the case studies in more detail. Following the interviews, post-interview discussions were conducted to focus on summarizing and cross validating the observations. The identified motivational/driving factors, input factors, and influencing factors were ranked by the managers of the respective firms. The "key/vital-few" factors identified are presented in Table 6.1. Additional archival data such as reports on public domains, including their Web sites and quality management records (ISO 9001, CMMI, COPC etc.,) maintained by the respective banks, and process excellence/business excellence award applications were also collected to help minimize any identified retrospective bias. A total of 62 interviews were conducted in the first round. The qualitative data analysis was then performed with a within-case analysis and then subsequently extended to a cross-case analysis (Miles et al. 1994). The additional relevant literature was incorporated at this stage to understand the emerging concepts, also provided an additional source of validation.

At this stage, the banks were again approached to obtain both, the operational and strategic orientations of their LSS programs. During these second-round interactions, managers were provided with an overview of the emerging themes, and their feedback about the emerging concepts was solicited. Multiple interactions with the informants also provided relevancy to the concepts and theory that emerged from this study. A total of 33 interviews were conducted as a part of the second-round interactions. These interviews also provided additional information about how these banks measured the actual outcomes of LSS deployment. For example, during the interviews, the managers were asked to describe their key metrics used for evaluating their LSS program. While analyzing the responses from "AA", it was found that a total of 42 LSS project opportunities were identified in the year-1, among which 32 ideas came from the managers, and the remaining ten were intellectual contributions from the frontline staff. Since "AA" was graduating from Lean to LSS, they prioritized 25 project cases (inclusive of all ten ideas from the frontline staff). 16 out of 25 LSS projects were successful in the year-1 and resulted in benefits worth USD 2.4 million. Further, the LSS projects delivered quality and productivity improvement, error reduction, and risk mitigation benefits. Strategic outcomes included creation of a knowledge pool of LSS practitioners, staff learning, and higher customer satisfaction (measured annually). These evaluation metrics were gathered at the end of each year across the three firms. A summary of these is presented in Table 6.1. Finally, 16 further interviews were conducted with representatives from banks' top management to further confirm the themes that emerged and to arrive at a level of theoretical saturation. The final step involved the cross-case analysis to establish the connection between the induced theoretical themes for measurement.

6.3 Approach to Study the Strategic Orientations

Table 6.1 Summary of interviews

		Bank-AA	Bank-BB	Bank-CC
Motivational drivers to embark upon LSS deployment	Key operational drivers	To • Generate higher cost efficiencies • Reduce process variation and defects • Improve responsiveness and customer satisfaction • Effect quality and productivity improvement • Establish a centralized project management function to enable CI • Compete with other market players	To • Realize breakthrough improvements and disruptive innovations • Increase revenue and reduce errors • Improve time-to-delivery to clients • Demonstrate effective risk management • Achieve process standardization across locations • Effect quality and productivity improvements	To • Enable and sustain continuous improvements • Integrate the existing Lean and Six Sigma programs • Enable rapidness and robustness in process improvement projects
	Key strategic drivers	To • Create a PI culture at the workplace • Realize customer value creation • Enable effective decision making using structured and analytical thinking	To • Improve competitiveness • Improve innovation quotient at workplace • Promote business excellence capability • Create a culture of process improvement at workplace	To • Promote employee ideation, participation, and recognition leading to improved staff morale • Enable knowledge management for continuous learning and process capabilities • Create a culture of CI
Input factors	Key organizational resources	• Highly motivated staff who are committed towards PI. A few of these staff are already trained in Lean methodology • Organizational dashboards, leadership and management information system • Lean Six Sigma Belts (professionals hired for LSS deployment) • In-house training and mentoring material and personnel • Statistical software for project-level analysis	• ISO:9001 audit documents, existing process maps, service-level agreements • Mid management staff who have voluntarily shown interest to take-up LSS projects • External consultants involved in LSS training and mentoring • Market research data (LSS deployment details and benchmarking data from other banks external to the firm)	• Existing Lean and Six Sigma projects • Lessons learned from earlier CI programs • Organizational databases and process information • Staff across all levels of the bank, irrespective of their position and role • Existing in-house LSS professionals and subject matter experts • Operations team leaders and management dashboards • Existing process management and statistical software
	Key organizational processes	• Existing Leaned processes in business functions, viz. mortgages, equities, forex, wealth management, cash investments and derivatives • Idea generation and evaluation process,	• Product-based transactional processes aligned with business priorities, viz. credit cards, traveler's cheques, commercial loans etc., • Training, sequencing, prioritizing,	• Idea generation, project identification process, training and coaching processes, project execution using DMAIC and DMADV methods, program governance, and leadership reporting

(continued)

Table 6.1 (continued)

		Bank-AA	Bank-BB	Bank-CC
		project execution using DMAIC methodology, program governance, and leadership reporting	presentation, data analysis and interpretation, project execution • Change management, communications and decision making, staff recognition	• Product-based transactional processes, viz. credit cards, fixed income, equity and trades, prime brokerage, cash management, trade finance, wealth management etc.,
	Key operational capabilities	• Transactional capability • Process management • Logistics management • Knowledge codification and coordination	• Vendor management • Process management • Escalation and client complaints management • Competitor analysis and market research capability	• Integration capability • Process management • Knowledge codification and coordination
Influencing factors	Key endogenous factors	• Effective communication • Leadership and management commitment • Effective use of technology • Organization structure • Measuring success and goal orientation • Employees' motivation, appetite for learning, reward and recognition system • Teamwork • Handling resistance to change • Stakeholders' management	• Training effectiveness • Teamwork and collaboration across organizational silos inside the firm • Employees' motivation triggers like recognition, rewards, visibility, learning opportunities, promoting competition • Ongoing evaluation, monitoring and assessment • Handling resistance to change • Organizational structure, beliefs, values, and priorities	• Realizing that process improvement is everyone's job • Top-down leadership and management involvement • Effective use of technology • Result orientation • Flexibility, agility, and commitment • Employee recognition • Involving customers as part of the LSS projects • Stakeholders' management
	Key exogenous factors	• Talent market at the location of the bank's center • Cross cultural management across different regional centers of the bank • Regulatory and economical dependencies	• Market practices and benchmarking data • Customer feedback • Marketability of LSS trained staff for career development	• Influence of external third-party consultants as an alternative to in-house LSS program • Marketability of LSS trained staff for career development • Social and regulatory factors

6.4 Findings from a Dynamic Capabilities' Perspective

While there are several theories of strategic management that could be used to study LSS in banks, we used dynamic capabilities' theory for this purpose. The nature of LSS as a DC is established through a cross-case analysis. The below sub-sections elaborate on the findings.

6.4.1 Compelling Need for Purposive Creation of LSS Capability

A 5-Why analysis of the motivational factors revealed that the primary driver to embark on the LSS journey is the banks' belief that LSS could lead to competitive advantage in quality. It was noted that this belief constitutes three ingredients, viz., (a) earlier experiences of the CI programs including Lean and Six Sigma, (b) influence of LSS success stories of other firms across different markets, and (c) their appetite towards creating a competitive advantage in quality. Hence, it is evident from all the three cases that *a compelling need to develop and sustain competitive advantage in quality drives firms to embark on the LSS journey*. Further, the presence of input factors shows that *LSS as a CI practice could be consciously created in firms by focused efforts and does not exist by mere chance*. These factors include organizational resources, processes and static routines (otherwise called as ordinary capabilities). These drivers and input factors were identified during our initial interviews. The motivational drivers were classified into operational drivers and strategic drivers and input factors as firm's resources, processes and ordinary capabilities. This validated our understanding and classification of these drivers and factors during the conversations with the top management. These were also refined through the interactions with the respondents.

6.4.2 LSS as a Vital Component of the Capabilities Network

From a systems perspective, organizations are complex systems with intertwined capabilities. Each of these capabilities is an element of a bundle (Barney 2001), which is part of a capabilities network. These capabilities influence or get influenced by other capabilities within as well as across different bundles and lead to the desired outcomes. According to Teece (2018), these influences among the capabilities contribute to a greater degree of dynamism of the capabilities network. Table 6.1 reveals the influencing factors experienced by the three banks as a part of their LSS journeys. This confirms that both internal and external environmental factors influence LSS and its functional attributes. For example, employee motivation and recognition identified as an influencing factor here is also recognized as a critical success factor in the literature (Albliwi et al. 2014). This means that employee motivation and recognition influence the success of LSS in its evolutionary path as well as in realizing the desired outcomes. In other words, the presence or absence of an influencing factor impacts both the direction (success or failure) and magnitude (low, medium or high) of the LSS outcomes. The magnitude of the influence of the concerned factor is further impacted by other organizational capabilities in the network. In the case of the above example, employee recognition and motivation which impacts LSS are further influenced by organization culture, rewards, and recognition system specific to the firm, leadership, etc. Other organizational capabilities that are a part of the bundle with LSS include project management, stakeholder's management, knowledge management, process management, etc. It is inferred that *LSS as an organizational capability needs to be nourished for progress, as it gets influenced by both internal and external factors of a firm.* Since, these influencing factors exist in networks, focused and diligent efforts are required towards nourishment of LSS. Failure stories of CI programs described in the literature provide strong evidence to support this proposition.

6.4.3 Path Dependency and Emergence

During our interactions with the managers of the banks, it was identified and validated that the paths the firms experienced before embarking upon their LSS journey have a critical impact on the progress. For example, "AA" which embarked upon Lean deployment before graduating to LSS maintained a knowledge repository of all their Lean projects. This helped them not to re-invent the solutions in many projects. Process improvement ideas which were implemented in one business unit were validated using variation analysis of the LSS toolkit in other business units. This helped them to filter the quick-wins, which continued to be Lean projects, from the other issues where root causes were unknown, as candidates for LSS. The path travelled by "AA" and the subsequent lessons learned helped them during their LSS deployment. Since "BB" had no background in Lean deployment, they took a different path to realize the benefits of LSS. Similarly, "CC" which had both Lean and Six Sigma as separate initiatives before embarking upon their LSS journey were aware of their past lessons and used them purposively. This helped them in their LSS progress. Hence, alongside the influencing factors that impact the progress of LSS in real-time, LSS capability exhibits dependency on the past knowledge trajectory of the firm and the decisions made. Hence, LSS capability is not limited by the current competence base. Similarly, the current knowledge base derived at any point in time serves as a strategic resource to the future actions leading to an emergence of learning as an ongoing process. In other words, *LSS exhibits path dependency and the emergence phenomenon.*

6.4.4 LSS Enables Organizational Learning

Path dependency is an attribute of past experiences and lessons learned, but organizational learning is a function of the rate of change in an organization's knowledge base that increases the range of its potential behaviors. The organizational learning process includes creating, acquiring, retaining, applying, and transferring knowledge within an organization over a period, and this could happen at various levels. Literature (Cheng and Van deVen 1996) shows that reactive actions like detecting and correcting errors are first-order learning. This predominantly characterizes refinement of existing processes for improvement and using the learning to multiply benefits across similar functional units in firms. Second-order learning includes understanding the underlying causes of problems towards discovering the standards and values behind actions and is characterized by experimentation, innovation, and exploration. Meta-learning, is a third type of learning that has not been discussed in the literature as relevant to CI (Ambrosini and Bowman 2009; Su et al. 2014). It refers to a firm's ability of "learning how to learn better" and its ability to systematically improve the first and second learning processes. Dynamic capabilities evolve from learning mechanisms, such as experience accumulation, knowledge articulation, and knowledge codification. While the DMAIC and DMADV approaches of LSS initiatives enable first-order and second-order learning, in our analysis of organizational data, it was evident that LSS is not merely about effecting process improvement or process design/re-redesign projects. It cannot be restricted to preventive or corrective actions or at a root causes analysis level of learning. LSS is an enabler of an organizational culture towards CI which is more than mere execution of a few improvement projects. The qualitative data analysis revealed that across the three banks, ideation of LSS candidates, implementation of LSS projects, and recognition for the outcomes of LSS deployment have enabled an organizational change in both tangible benefits and behaviors of employees. Managers recognized the fact that LSS experience has changed the way their staff see or think about the processes and systems. Questioning the status quo of the processes, rather than following a routine standard operating procedure; brainstorming for creative ideas to deliver value to clients with less resources; frontline staff realizing the importance of shifting their focus towards customer centricity; statistical validation of intuitive ideas or opinions, etc., are a few of the examples which were gauged in the interviews with managers and further validated during our site visits. Thus, *LSS contributes to the organizational learning process in firms, due to its ability to contribute towards first-order (exploitative/reactive) learning, second-order (explorative/proactive) learning, and meta learning (learning to learn) for creating a culture of CI on an ongoing basis.*

6.4.5 Technical and Evolutionary Fitness of LSS

While examining the total cost of the LSS deployment and the returns it delivered across the study period, it is evident that "AA" and "CC" broke-even within a few months of their LSS implementation and enjoyed consistent benefits. "BB" realized their break-even in year 2. The ROI percentages of all the three banks at the end of three years were promising and ranged between 200 and 400%. Further, the operational benefits delivered by the LSS capability across different organizational metrics like ideas generated, ideas to projects ratio, project wise benefits, etc., determine its working potential. Further, operational metrics like cycle time, customer satisfaction rate, first time resolution rate, net promoter score, process yield, error percentage in delivery, risk reduction, etc., and strategic measures including employee morale, building a culture of CI, enabling the right balance in bottom-up and top-down expectations for change management, were encouraging. This is evidence that LSS fulfilled its intended function in the banks. However, while comparing the three banks, it was interesting to note that "CC" accomplished the above benefits quicker than the other two because of its experience in implementing Lean and Six Sigma separately before integrating them into LSS. They utilized existing resources and did not hire external LSS professionals for deployment. This enabled the existing staff, who had already demonstrated their experience in previous CI projects using Lean/Six Sigma, to play a leadership role in LSS deployment. This enabled easier change management, boosted staff morale, and eliminated the cost of hiring external LSS professionals. Though "AA" had past Lean deployment experience, LSS was new to them. Due to the implementation of LSS, the concerned staff members developed a sense of being differentiated within the bank. Specifically, the staff who were not involved in the LSS projects belonging to the first set of cohorts felt left out. Intriguingly, such a feeling of being differentiated prevailed even among the staff constituting the implementation teams. This happened because of the belting system, which led a few of the staff to presume and assert their superiority in their roles as change agents. Naturally, the remaining staff felt that they were lower down the LSS implementation pecking order. Consequently, there was a noticeable resistance among them towards the entire initiative. In order to address these issues, the bank hired external LSS experts to create awareness and train the existing staff in the LSS Green Belt program. In year 2, a few highly capable Green Belts were trained to attain the Black Belt level for creating the LSS capability in the natural functional teams. However, even this move was not appreciated by some of the staff members. The belting system did not provide an opportunity to all the staff to contribute to CI at the same level, despite many of them having evinced interest. To address this confusion, the top management of "AA" dismissed the belting system, customized their LSS nomenclature, and rebranded their LSS program as "Lean Six Sigma Practitioner program." They realized the intended purpose of LSS by the end of year 2. Similarly, "BB" contracted external consultants to train and mentor LSS projects executed by their staff. With no prior formal CI program, the staff of "BB" experienced a fresh and exciting LSS journey towards the realization of its intended purpose. Though the pace and magnitude of benefiting from LSS were different across the three banks, it was observed that LSS reconfigured their resource base by creating, extending, and modifying various processes and systems, with a direct positive impact on both customers and employees. According to Helfat (2007), a capability that exhibits and measures up to its "technical fitness" and "evolutionary fitness" qualifies to be called a DC. The first, technical fitness, denotes how effectively a capability performs its intended function when normalized (divided) by its cost. The second, evolutionary fitness, refers to how well a DC enables an organization to improve by creating, extending, or modifying its resource base (Helfat and Peteraf 2009). Hence, *LSS exhibits both technical and evolutionary fitness.*

6.4.6 LSS Exhibits VRIN Characteristics

DCs are a source of sustained competitive advantage in firms. Barney (1991) defines competitive advantage as the degree to which a firm has reduced costs and exploited opportunities. Many scholars have employed a "resource heterogeneity approach," which states that a sustained competitive advantage can be conceptualized as the degree of four features abbreviated as VRIN: Value, Rareness, Inimitability, and Non-substitutability.

Value: The operational and strategic benefits that LSS capability demonstrated across the three banks to all groups of stakeholders (customers, employees, and organizational systems) towards both process improvement and process redesign justify its value potential. For example, during our interactions, one manager mentioned that "LSS provided breakthrough improvements in our processes. A few of the solutions which emerged from LSS projects include introduction of chat for client interactions, thus helping us move away from our erstwhile call center model and standardizing our transaction monitoring across eight countries, over a period of 18 months." Another manager acknowledged the value addition of LSS by saying "The LSS deployment helped us to continuously revisit our resources and processes and discover where we can improve, as a value-enabler to our business transformation." Further, the fact that it was a significant contributor to build a culture of CI, which further has several positive impacts (like improving quality, customer centricity, agility at work, etc.,) at the workplace, reveals the "value" of LSS.

Rareness: This feature is defined as how much of a firm's LSS resources and capabilities are not possessed by its competitors. Measuring rareness must account for the degree to which a firm exploits its unique resources, processes and capabilities, and their combinations. The fact that LSS enabled employees to ideate for process improvements using their transactional and cognitive capabilities denotes its rareness. Additionally, LSS's differentiated training enhances traditional quality training in firms. The amount and content of training for different levels of staff are tailored to match the complexity of tasks and to increase their other capabilities for solving complex problems, innovation, knowledge management, etc., all of which help to challenge the status-quo and increase the impact of CI. During the site visits, it was found that every LSS project focused on finding the root causes of lower performance levels and generating subsequent ideas for improvement through brainstorming sessions. This enabled innovation and the generation of distinct ideas for both incremental and breakthrough improvements. Classification and prioritization tools like Fishbone diagram, Affinity diagram, and Control-impact matrix helped in categorization of both, the root causes and their associated improvement ideas. Further, these were measured to indicate rareness levels objectively. One manager who endorsed our observations said "LSS educated our managers to look at business problems using both process and data lenses leading to improved process metrics, viz. cost reduction, productivity improvement, etc., and every project was unique." Further, rareness was observed across many phases of LSS deployment, viz. project selection, execution, training, certification practices, etc.

Inimitability: Existence of common features among effective DCs does not however imply that a specific one is exactly alike across firms (Eisenhardt and Martin 2000). LSS deployment in a firm requires distinctive and consciously developed practices and processes. These organizational practices and processes often display high levels of coherence, and when they do, replication may be difficult because it requires systemic changes throughout the organization and also among inter-organizational linkages, which might be very hard to imitate (Teece et al. 1997). Further, Teece et al. (1994, 1997) claimed that partial imitation of a capability or replication of a successful deployment model may yield zero benefits. Each of the three banks studied here had several commonalities in terms of the nature of resources and processes. Each of their LSS capabilities stood distinctly due to path dependencies and attributes of organization culture (values, beliefs, administrative methods, etc.), which were found predominantly tacit, hence making replication and imitation very difficult. This created unique systemic differences among the banks with regards to their LSS drivers, input factors, influencing factors, approaches, and outcomes.

Non-substitutability: The rapidness of Lean and robustness of Six Sigma toolkits and their synergies constituted LSS (Sunder M 2013, Sunder M et al. 2018). AA, which embarked upon their LSS journey after successful deployment of Lean for two years, saw unique value in LSS. For example, a manager of the bank claimed that "Though we faced challenges in change management during our graduation from Lean to LSS, we must agree that LSS helped in the renewal of our existing Lean program." Similarly, "CC", which had experience in Lean and Six Sigma separately before deploying LSS, also found LSS more valuable than Lean and Six Sigma in isolation. Hence, Lean and Six Sigma cannot be substitutes for LSS, which results from their synergy. Despite the argument that contemporary socio-technical practices like process automation could substitute the intended purpose of LSS, our study revealed that LSS could only supplement such efficiency creation initiatives and cannot be perceived as a competition or a substitute. For example, one manager responded during an interview, "While we have plans to deploy Agile and Robotics in the medium term, we believe that LSS has laid a platform to first improve the processes before automating them."

6.4.7 LSS Exhibits Agility Towards Environmental Dynamism

In the context of business organizations, environmental dynamism represents the rate of change in the organizational environment. When the environment is relatively stable with no significant technological progress or only a few customer preferences changes, LSS becomes expensive. However, in volatile environments,

LSS makes significant contributions to enable the organizational processes and systems to align with the changes. LSS makes this through a structured approach manifested through a well-integrated and sequenced set of projects that make change management easier. This aligns well with Juran's (1989) pointer that "improvement happens project-by-project and in no other way." From an external environmental perspective, it is evident from our study that LSS helped managers to bring in new trends and perspectives from the market, both from customer interactions and from market research. For example, one bank reported that LSS helped them to adopt a new channel in their post-sales service desk processes. They implemented a chat channel, which they found to be more effective and less expensive compared to the traditional call center approach. Another LSS project aimed at employee upskilling to create opportunities for change management in a structured way. In another project which aimed to reduce customer complaints, customer requirements changed in the middle of the project journey, but still, the project delivered on the new expectations. The project manager attributed this success to a few LSS tools such as the Kano model, FMEA, and the Pugh matrix, which she believed enabled agility and customer centricity. In another such project, it was observed that the project team used QFD to gather the evolving customer requirements aligned with the banking product's characteristics. During site visits, it was observed that LSS keeps the knowledge flow aligned with the changes in the environment as LSS tools enable customer centricity and agility towards driving the desired outcomes. Even from an internal environment perspective, it was found that LSS enables organizational agility. The organizational records provided evidence that LSS complimented other existing organizational practices like ISO, benchmarking, some customer satisfaction realization methods, training and development, employee engagement and recognition, etc. Rather than creating a new cult, LSS fitted into the organizational ecosystems enhancing the existing quality practices by boosting-in structured problem-solving capability, alongside delivering on its intended purpose. From the case evidence, it can be stated that *LSS exhibits agility towards environmental dynamism.*

6.5 Summary of This Chapter

Previous studies in CI have argued that the complex interactions of various quality practices lead to an effective quality system that would be difficult to replicate by competitors. Through this chapter, we challenge the traditional view of CI by managing static resources and routines. It is the dynamic maneuvering that creates a series of temporary advantages to help organizations create and sustain new forms of quality advantage over time. In contrast, this study advocates the DCs approach as a counterintuitive model to this thinking. This study has evaluated LSS, a contemporary CI practice, using an iterative triangulation method to reflect its strategic value towards creating competitive advantage in quality. It differs from previous studies by specifying that LSS is not merely a CI practice, but a higher-order organizational capability, more precisely a DC, towards creating competitive advantage in quality.

References

Albliwi, S., Antony, J., Abdul Halim Lim, S., & van der Wiele, T. (2014). Critical failure factors of Lean Six Sigma: A systematic literature review. *International Journal of Quality & Reliability Management, 31*(9), 1012–1030.
Ambrosini, V., & Bowman, C. (2009). What are dynamic capabilities and are they a useful construct in strategic management? *International journal of management reviews, 11*(1), 29–49.
Amit, R., & Schoemaker, P. J. (1993). Strategic assets and organizational rent. *Strategic Management Journal, 14*(1), 33–46.
Anand, G., Ward, P. T., Tatikonda, M. V., & Schilling, D. A. (2009). Dynamic capabilities through continuous improvement infrastructure. *Journal of operations management, 27*(6), 444–461.
Barney, J. (1991). Special theory forum the resource-based model of the firm: Origins, implications, and prospects. *Journal of Management, 17*(1), 97–98.
Barney, J. B. (2001). Resource-based theories of competitive advantage: A ten-year retrospective on the resource-based view. *Journal of Management, 27*(6), 643–650.
Cheng, Y. T., & Van de Ven, A. H. (1996). Learning the innovation journey: Order out of chaos? *Organization Science, 7*(6), 593–614.
Collis, D. J. (1994). Research note: How valuable are organizational capabilities? *Strategic Management Journal, 15*(S1), 143–152.
Danneels, E. (2002). The dynamics of product innovation and firm competences. *Strategic Management Journal, 23*(12), 1095–1121.
Dobrzykowski, D. D., McFadden, K. L., & Vonderembse, M. A. (2016). Examining pathways to safety and financial performance in hospitals: A study of lean in professional service operations. *Journal of Operations Management, 42,* 39–51.
Douglas, T. J., & Judge, W. Q., Jr. (2001). Total quality management implementation and competitive advantage: The role of structural control and exploration. *Academy of Management Journal, 44*(1), 158–169.
Eisenhardt, K. M., & Martin, J. A. (2000). Dynamic capabilities: What are they? *Strategic Management Journal, 21*(10–11), 1105–1121.
Grant, R. M. (1991). The resource-based theory of competitive advantage: Implications for strategy formulation. *California Management Review, 33*(3), 114–135.
Heimeriks, G. (2012). Interdisciplinarity in biotechnology, genomics and nanotechnology. *Science and Public Policy, 40*(1), 97–112.
Helfat, C. E. (2007). Stylized facts, empirical research and theory development in management. *Strategic Organization, 5,* 185–192.
Helfat, C. E., & Peteraf, M. A. (2003). The dynamic resource-based view: Capability lifecycles. *Strategic Management Journal, 24*(10), 997–1010.
Helfat, C. E., & Peteraf, M. A. (2009). Understanding dynamic capabilities: Progress along a developmental path. *Strategic Organization, 7,* 91–102.
Helfat, C. E., Finkelstein, S., Mitchell, W., Peteraf, M. A., Singh, H., Teece, D. J., & Winter, S. G. (2007). *Dynamic capabilities: foundations. Dynamic capabilities: Understanding strategic change in organizations* (pp. 30–45).
Hine, D., Parker, R., Pregelj, L., & Verreynne, M. L. (2013). Deconstructing and reconstructing the capability hierarchy. *Industrial and Corporate Change, 23*(5), 1299–1325.
Itami, H. (1981). *Roehl, 1987, Mobilizing invisible assets.*

References

Juran, J. M. (1989). *Juran on leadership for quality: An executive handbook*. New York: Free Press.

Learned, E. P. (1969). *Business policy: Text and cases*. RD Irwin.

Miles, M. B., Huberman, A. M., Huberman, M. A., & Huberman, M. (1994). *Qualitative data analysis: An expanded sourcebook*. Sage.

Nelson, R. R., & Winter, S. G. (1973). Toward an evolutionary theory of economic capabilities. *The American Economic Review, 63*(2), 440–449.

Prahalad, C. K., & Hamel, G. (1990). Core competency concept. *Harvard Business Review, 64*(3), 70–92.

Protogerou, A., Caloghirou, Y., & Lioukas, S. (2011). Dynamic capabilities and their indirect impact on firm performance. *Industrial and Corporate Change, 21*(3), 615–647.

Schilke, O., Hu, S., & Helfat, C. E. (2018). Quo vadis, dynamic capabilities? A content-analytic review of the current state of knowledge and recommendations for future research. *Academy of Management Annals, 12*(1), 390–439.

Schreyögg, G., & Kliesch-Eberl, M. (2007). How dynamic can organizational capabilities be? Towards a dual-process model of capability dynamization. *Strategic Management Journal, 28*(9), 913–933.

Su, H. C., Linderman, K., Schroeder, R. G., & Van de Ven, A. H. (2014). A comparative case study of sustaining quality as a competitive advantage. *Journal of Operations Management, 32*(7–8), 429–445.

Sunder M, V. (2013). Synergies of lean six sigma. *IUP Journal of Operations Management, 12*(1), 21.

Sunder M, V., Ganesh, L. S., & Marathe, R. R. (2018). A morphological analysis of research literature on Lean Six Sigma for services. *International Journal of Operations & Production Management, 38*(1), 149–182.

Sunder M, V., Ganesh, L.S. & Marathe, R. R. (2019). Dynamic capabilities: A morphological analysis framework and agenda for future research. *European Business Review, 31*(1), 25–63.

Teece, D. J. (2007). Explicating dynamic capabilities: The nature and microfoundations of (sustainable) enterprise performance. *Strategic Management Journal, 28*(13), 1319–1350.

Teece, D. J. (2014). The foundations of enterprise performance: Dynamic and ordinary capabilities in an (economic) theory of firms. *Academy of Management Perspectives, 28*(4), 328–352.

Teece, D. J. (2018). Business models and dynamic capabilities. *Long Range Planning, 51*(1), 40–49.

Teece, D., & Pisano, G. (1994). The dynamic capabilities of firms: an introduction. *Industrial and Corporate Change, 3*(3), 537–556.

Teece, D., & Pisano, G. (2003). The dynamic capabilities of firms. In *Handbook on knowledge management* (pp. 195–213). Berlin: Springer.

Teece, D. J., Pisano, G., & Shuen, A. (1997). Dynamic capabilities and strategic management. *Strategic Management Journal, 18*(7), 509–533.

Winter, S. G. (2003). Understanding dynamic capabilities. *Strategic Management Journal, 24*(10), 991–995.

Witcher, B. J., Sum Chau, V., & Harding, P. (2008). Dynamic capabilities: Top executive audits and hoshin kanri at Nissan South Africa. *International Journal of Operations & Production Management, 28*(6), 540–561.

Zahra, S. A., Sapienza, H. J., & Davidsson, P. (2006). Entrepreneurship and dynamic capabilities: A review, model and research agenda. *Journal of Management Studies, 43*(4), 917–955.

Zollo, M., & Winter, S. G. (2002). Deliberate learning and the evolution of dynamic capabilities. *Organization Science, 13*(3), 339–351.

Summary and Conclusions 7

LSS has emerged as an essential part of CI in services by providing several valuable outcomes. From a ST perspective, LSS is not merely a combination of Lean and Six Sigma, but a synergetic hybrid approach for effecting transformational change in organizations. Alongside improving customer and employee satisfaction, LSS also strives to reduce costs and manage risk in services firms. This book highlighted the operational and strategic importance of LSS for creating competitive advantage in firms. The strategic orientation of organizational capabilities and related dynamic capability theory were applied through case evidence beyond the operational benefits that LSS could deliver.

Firstly, the importance of DCs and a need to examine the associated literature were justified. Then, competitive advantage in quality has been studied. Amidst the quality management literature, the book examined the concept of CI. It was interesting to learn the applicability of Lean and Six Sigma as two most widely used CI practices. It was evident from the literature of Lean and Six Sigma that they have both successes and criticisms.

A systematic literature review provided directions for future research on this topic through the morphological analysis technique. Four types of classifications of the literature, viz. fundamental, methodological, chronological, and sector-wise, were presented. Further, a systematic review of 175 scholarly papers from 67 journals enabled the presentation of the MA framework. A total of 355 research gaps were identified as an outcome of this exercise. It was evident that the current academic research on LSS in services is limited and hence reinforces a need for deeper research. Three hundred and fifty-five research gaps identified in this book serve as a resource for scholars to embark their future research on the topic of LSS.

Then, an examination of *LSS projects in banking firms* using a case-based approach is presented. By studying LSS project cases from two banks (optimization of employee utilization and accuracy improvement in payments processing), lessons learned and implications were highlighted. It was concluded that the extent of applicability of LSS in BFS depends on the interest, rigor, and scope of the banking operations. It is further concluded that LSS project management is merely a subset of LSS deployment in banks. Both tangible and intangible benefits of LSS are evident in the banking context from the above two real-world case evidences. Further research is needed to strengthen the understanding of LSS from the process, human and culture perspectives in BFS organizations. It is concluded that LSS needs to be understood using a systemic perspective in order to move away from a narrow project-only approach. An LSS project selection criterion was recommended. This framework will help managers to select correct and appropriate opportunities for CI. Further, important managerial implications were discovered (Sunder M 2016). These include effective management of stakeholders and change leadership as essential elements of LSS project management in banks.

This book has not only looked at LSS merely from a project management perspective for deriving practical managerial implications but has also provided an examination of LSS deployment. While the previous studies in CI represented quality management through various practices (for operational benefits) and argued that the complex interactions of CI practices lead to an effective quality system, this book challenged this traditional view and advocated the DCs approach as a counterintuitive model. It has established *LSS as a DC* using longitudinal case evidence. Using an iterative triangulation method to reflect its strategic value toward creating competitive advantage in quality, this book evaluated LSS to be recognized as a DC for strategy applications. Using a purposive sample of three global banks, the primary data was collected using multiple rounds of interviews with select top- and mid-management personnel, site visits, participation in LSS project meetings and execution, study of management archives and reported data on public domains. For triangulation, this primary data was synthesized with the results noted from the research literature on both LSS and DCs, which were studied independently by previous researchers. A cross-comparison of the case studies was performed to derive useful propositions that have been used to build a conceptual model. Then, LSS was evaluated on its technical and evolutionary fitness. Finally, this book presented ten characteristics of LSS that confirm it to be management strategy and not merely a CI practice. As a management strategy, LSS helps top management in decision making, promoting innovation and enabling organizational capabilities.

While the case data used for presentation of this book comes from the banking sector, the findings and results presented here have applicability beyond BFS. This book explored many avenues, implications, and frameworks to advance the body of knowledge of both LSS, DCs and their novel integration. We believe that this book will help both practitioners and researchers to realize the value of LSS as a strategic resource for holistic benefits beyond its operational applications and a platform to advance the potential research, respectively.

Reference

Sunder M, V. (2016). Lean Six Sigma project management—a stakeholder management perspective. *The TQMJournal, 28*(1), 132–150.

GPSR Compliance

The European Union's (EU) General Product Safety Regulation (GPSR) is a set of rules that requires consumer products to be safe and our obligations to ensure this.

If you have any concerns about our products, you can contact us on

ProductSafety@springernature.com

In case Publisher is established outside the EU, the EU authorized representative is:

Springer Nature Customer Service Center GmbH
Europaplatz 3
69115 Heidelberg, Germany

www.ingramcontent.com/pod-product-compliance
Lightning Source LLC
LaVergne TN
LVHW012247070526
838201LV00091B/152